R2D2 LIVES IN PRESTON

THE BEST OF BBC 6 MUSIC'S
TOAST THE NATION!

R2D2
LIVES IN
PRESTON

SHAUN KEAVENY

BBC RADIO 6 music

BOXTREE

First published 2010 by Boxtree
an imprint of Pan Macmillan, a division of Macmillan Publishers Limited
Pan Macmillan, 20 New Wharf Road, London N1 9RR
Basingstoke and Oxford
Associated companies throughout the world
www.panmacmillan.com

ISBN 978-0-7522-2745-0

1 3 5 7 9 8 6 4 2

A CIP catalogue record for this book is available from
the British Library.

Printed in the UK by CPI Mackays, Chatham ME5 8TD

This book is dedicated to the remarkable,
ingenious, industrious, hilarious, but most of all
wonderfully loyal and loving listeners of Six Music
without whom it would never have survived.

Contents

INTRODUCTION

As you flip absentmindedly through this tome in the bookshop, fish fingers slowly defrosting in the shopping bag betwixt your ankles, you may well be asking the question: 'What the f**k *is* this "Toast the Nation"? What does it all mean? And why did I buy fish fingers? What am I, twelve?'

Well, I can't help you with the penultimate question (except to say you are not alone: fish fingers are proper delicious!) but I can with the other two. Toast the Nation (or TTN) was a feature on my BBC 6 Music radio show for a long time, and its premise was very simple. Each day we invited a listener to our bijou but perfectly formed national breakfast show to extol the virtues of their town/city/village/hamlet by hitting us with some little-known/uncorroborated facts about the area, some musical heritage (we *are* the nation's premier alt-music station after all) and, to finish, a song that would be in some way – HOWEVER TENUOUSLY – linked to said place.

A simple premise, therefore, but one that gripped the national imagination so tightly by the windpipe that the British Isles went blue for a bit and nearly passed out. Why people loved it so, we can only speculate. Our hunch, after much cogitation, is that people love taking the piss, and getting their favourite song played on the radio.

The quintessential Nation Toaster managed to uniquely combine a sense of civic pride with an unstinting eye for the pathetic and absurd minutiae of parochial life. Every Toaster

****

had come to accept the surroundings they, sometimes begrudgingly, called home, often much like a partner would accept their husband or wife in a harmonious but unfulfilling marriage.

The result is a whirligig of wondrous facts about some of the most insalubrious places in the British Isles. Who knew for instance that what's known as the Magic Roundabout in Swindon is the seventh most feared road junction in Britain? Or that Weymouth has the largest seagulls in the world – so big they've been known to swoop down and snatch small children? I know what you're thinking – how could I have lived without such information?

These are examples of exactly what is to be found within this volume. And let this serve as a warning: if you require a book to change your view of the world forever and provide a new philosophical prism through which to view your place in the universe, pop this down and have a go at that Albert Camus novel you've always wanted to get round to finishing. On the other hand, if you can't really be arsed with Camus, but would be fascinated to discover that Northampton has the world's first and only lift-testing facility, READ ON!

TOAST

SOUTH OF

ENGLAND

READING

Many a folk tale invokes the theme of the innocent knave who goes to the big city only to be seduced and ultimately corrupted by its nefarious charms. The story of my early life is no different. For me, the big city in question was, well actually not *technically* a city, it was Reading. That was where I TORE IT UP! OFF THE LEASH AND ON THE RAMPAGE FOR THE FIRST TIME AS A REAL LIVE ADULT! OK, it's not New York or Rio, but for me it held as much dangerous lure and promise as Tony Montana's Miami in *Scarface*.

Unlike Tony I never saw a fellow drug dealer's arm get sawn off. Nor did I ever snort from a kilo of cocaine whilst blasting the windows of my studio flat out with an M16. No. But I *did* get bladdered fortnightly in the excellent indie club After Dark. I also had many an excellent chicken korai in the Khukuri on London Street. I never killed a man but I did once see quite a bad fist fight in a kebab queue near the Purple Turtle. I admit this is not necessarily the stuff of a Hollywood blockbuster starring Al Pacino, but these are the memories that first spring to mind when discussing the great Berkshire conurbation of Reading.

Our two Reading Toasters, Emma and Duncan, give us a great breadth of top factage, from the obvious (the Winslet link), to the obscure (who knew Dickens was almost a local MP!), But my favourite fact about the place (not mentioned by Emma or Duncan) is that there is a division of OTIS lifts that operates in the town, which means that when the employees answer the telephone they are required to announce, 'Hello, Otis Reading.' Which appeals very much to my sense of humour. Or lack thereof.

```
TOASTERS: EMMA WALSH
          DUNCAN ATKINSON
```

Playlist

▷ **Yeah Yeah Yeahs** – Gold Lion

▷ **Chemical Brothers** – The Boxer

> **SHAUN SEZ:** When I first moved down south
> I lived in Reading where I met my first
> radio boss. He was an Australian who
> shall remain nameless (and clueless),
> who, despite years in the music business,
> still insisted on calling the Chemical
> Brothers the Chemistry Brothers. If
> brains were dynamite he wouldn't have
> enough to blow his cap off.

FAVOURITE FACTS

- Reading is famous (at least locally) for the three Bs:
  Beer: Simonds Brewery began here in 1785 and was
  eventually taken over by Courage.
  Bulbs: Suttons Seeds was founded in Reading in
  1806 and remained in Reading till 1976 (then relocated
  to Devon).
  Biscuits: The Huntley and Palmers factory was in central
  Reading and also provided the bar scenes in *Bugsy
  Malone* in 1975 just before production stopped in 1976.

****

- Reading Festival has been running since 1971, but we can't even claim that as our own any more; we have to share it with Leeds!

- Ricky Gervais (who comes from Reading) turned local town Whitley into a household name by describing the residents as the lowest members of society.

- Reading Prison was where Oscar Wilde served two years' hard labour for gross indecency; after his release he wrote *The Ballad of Reading Gaol*. It's now a Youth Offenders Institute.

- The roadside chain of restaurants Little Chef was founded in Reading in 1958 with an eleven-seater restaurant.

- Charles Dickens was asked to stand as MP for Reading – he declined.

- Richard Cox grew the first Cox's apple nearby.

- Local stately home Mapledurham House is said to be what the original illustrations of Toad Hall were based on.

- Reading is where the oldest recorded British song, 'Sumer is icumen in', was written in 1260. You can listen to it on Wikipedia. It's dire. But it is also, apparently, the tune the mice sing to in *Bagpuss*.

LOCAL HEROES

★ Kate Winslet is from Reading, and her dad plays in a local band.

★ Will Young and Chris Tarrant were also born here.

★ Kenneth Branagh moved to Reading aged nine to escape Belfast.

★ Ricky Gervais

★ Jane Austen attended the Abbey School in Reading.

★ Pete & The Pirates are from Reading.

★ Mike Oldfield

★ Not sure if this counts but there's a building called Kate Bush House, a house in Theale (where I live) just outside Reading.

★ Scott Wilkinson and Martin Noble of British Sea Power attended Reading University, as did Jamie Cullum.

★ Tom Rowlands (The Chemical Brothers) went to Reading Blue Coat School.

WEST WALWORTH

Have you ever had an over-friendly animal make its way into your house? According to Toaster Rebecca, it's the kind of thing that happens all the time in the Exo-London suburb of West Walworth. By her account, urban foxes are so brazen these days they'll 'come into the living room if you leave the door open'. (N.B. I find that I often bastardize the phrase 'urban fox' into 'urbane fox' and imagine them in cravats and mustard cords, swilling expensive cognac while they rip your bins to bits.) I had a similar thing happen to me once when I lived in Finsbury Park. Within days of moving into a new flat, I noticed a cute little cat visiting my minuscule patio area. I assumed she was missing titbits left by the previous occupier, and though it's my general cat-related rule *not* to feed a stray, I did just that, worn down by the voluminous displays of affection the minx directed at me.

Before long I was totally in her thrall, going out of my way to buy expensive pieces of fish to secure my place in her capricious heart. But, as cats so often do, she eventually lost interest and stopped coming altogether. I never even knew her name. What was worse was that, shortly after, I noticed large sums of money leaving my account. The lesson of this tale is clear: a) never give a cat your bank account details no matter how much you feel you can trust them; and b) cats are more intelligent than dogs.

Thanks also to Rebecca for letting us know that the man widely credited with the invention of the first computer, Charles Babbage, was a Walworth boy. Herein lies a lesson about the ravages of history. Though Babbage's inventions and discoveries have undoubtedly revolutionized history forever, paving the way to our hi-tech twenty-first-century internet-connected planet, it seems, in this country at least, he will instead be remembered as the name of the scoreboard on vapid Vernon Kaye vehicle *Family Fortunes*. Bummer!

TOASTER: REBECCA

Playlist

▷ **Stereo MCs** – Get Connected

FAVOURITE FACTS

➤ The Walworth Jumpers (or Children of God, Girlingites or Convulsionists) were a cult created by Mary Ann Girling in the 1870s in England. Born in Suffolk, Girling preached the Second Coming, celibacy, chastity and communal life (a kind of Christian communism). In 1871, the Children of God were invited to London by another new religious movement, the Peculiar People of Plumstead. They gathered around the railway arches of Walworth Road.

➤ My next-door neighbour seems to personify Walworth. He's a raving lunatic – though lovely and very friendly. He's a Mauritian in his sixties, living alone with his cats, some foxes, a radio for racing commentary and many bottles of red wine for company. He claims his flat is a 'safe house' and he's in hiding from the mob, and he gets up to various things such as: trying to sell porn to the gas man visiting my flat; sweetly passing us terrifying-looking curries over the fence that we can't bring ourselves to eat (and I eat pretty much anything); sleeping with a gun under his pillow; having a garden densely packed with fig trees to 'keep the asbos and oiks out'; and being seen only in two outfits – a wine-red dressing gown, with nowt underneath I fear, and a sharp suit for his weekly outings to the races.

- East Street Market in Walworth was established in 1880 and about a hundred years later was featured in the *Only Fools and Horses* titles.

- The foxes round here are so brazen, they'll come in the living room if you leave the door open.

LOCAL HEROES

★ Charlie Chaplin was born on 16 April 1889, in East Street, Walworth, London. His parents were both entertainers in the music-hall tradition; they separated before Charlie was three.

★ Michael Caine

★ Robert Browning

★ John Ruskin

★ Charles Babbage

★ Michael Faraday

★ Naomi Campbell

★ Nick Hallam, also known as 'The Head' from Stereo MCs.

★ Stuart Zender – Jamiroquai bassist.

★ Mark Ronson

****

FARINGDON

Playlist

▷ **Specials** – Rat Race (because people escape the rat race and move to Faringdon)

FAVOURITE FACTS

- Faringdon is in West Oxfordshire between Oxford and Swindon. It featured in the Domesday Book, and there's a market in town every week that's been running since the thirteenth century.

- Faringdon is the location of the last folly built in England. (A 'folly' is a building made just for decoration, and for no other use – except to duck out of the rain beneath, maybe.) Lord Berners, who built the folly in question, was so eccentric he put a sign on it saying 'Those who commit suicide from this high place do so entirely at their own risk.' He also dyed his pigeons bright colours and he is rumoured to have thrown his mum's dog out of the window as a child (he heard that a dog will learn to swim if you throw it in the water, so figured it would learn to fly if you threw it out of the window).

- The hill with the folly on was used as a hill fort in ancient times. Cromwell used it as a base to bombard the town from. As a result of this bombardment the

****

church (All Saints) in Faringdon has no steeple because it was blown away. After the war the parish got enough money together to rebuild the steeple, but the vicar drank it all. They say that the church is since haunted by the ghost of a drunk vicar.

LOCAL HEROES

★ Keith Floyd used to live in Faringdon.

★ Rory Bremner, Jason Donovan and Graham Coxon all live nearby.

CHISWICK

Chiswick. It's one of those words. Chiswick. The more you look at it, the weirder it gets. Here it is again. CHISWICK. *Chizz Wick!*

Anyway, where was I? Oh yes, CHIZZ WICK. Toastee Mary sets the scene by basically describing Chiswick as 'the eighth most expensive place to live in Britain' and 'a bit jolly hockey sticks'. I can corroborate this. As a now naturalized Londoner, I live only a stone's throw away, yet could never in a million years hope to rub shoulders with the likes of Ant, Dec, Bill Bailey and Bruce Dickinson. The immutable laws of commerce have damned me forever to live in a less leafy and desirable postcode, surrounded by other dead-eyed and desperate foundlings who can only dream of convening in Chiswick High Road's chic and celeb-engorged taverns, restaurants and tapas bars. My wife has repeatedly requested that I remove the giant sticker on the back of our house which says 'MY OTHER HOUSE IS IN CHISWICK', but her pleas have fallen on deaf ears.

Maybe I should give up on the idea of living in Chiswick. After all, I might end up being in the house that separates Ant from Dec. I have it on good authority that the plaintive whale-like whelps and cries they emit to call each other in the night are enough to drive anyone to self-harm.

TOASTER: MARY SWEENEY

Playlist

▷ **The Who** – Who Are You (Pete Townshend was born in Chiswick)

▷ **The Firm** – Star Trekking (Patrick Stewart used to live in Chiswick)

▷ **Airpushers** – Chiswick High Road (a funky little number that actually sounds nothing like Chiswick High Road, which is actually rather sedate and raaaaah, dahhhlink)

FAVOURITE FACTS

- The name 'Chiswick' is of Old English origin and means 'Cheese Farm'. Make of that what you will.

- In 2007 it was named the eighth most expensive place to live in the UK. It is a bit 'jolly hockey sticks' around here, I must admit.

- Chiswick features in many music videos, including those for 'Paperback Writer'by The Beatles, 'Roses For The Dead' by Funeral For A Friend, 'Dean' by Dizzee Rascal and 'Fit But You Know It' by The Streets.

- It also features in a notable number of TV sitcoms as the place where the main characters live: the Porters from *2point4 Children* lived in Chiswick; the family in *My Family* live in Chiswick; Donna (Catherine Tate) from *Doctor Who* is from Chiswick; and eighties sitcom *Three Up, Two Down* was set in Chiswick.

****

LOCAL HEROES

★ Ant and Dec live here – presumably separately, and not together.

★ James Dean Bradfield

★ William Hogarth (artist) – there's a statue of him on Chiswick High Road.

★ Bruce Dickinson

★ Bill Bailey

CROUCH END

Of all the major conurbations in this United Kingdom of ours, predictably, it's London that houses the most celebrities. For my money, one little hilly hamlet in the north of London grabs the title of 'district with most celebrities per square mile', and it's Crouch End, or *Crouche Ende* (say in a French accent) as it's more commonly known to the commoners who can't afford to live there.

I once was one such a commoner, who lived in nearby-but-not-quite-Crouch-End Hornsey. I would often wander the winding, tree-lined avenues to the hamlet's little heart and stare agog at the sheer volume of A-grade TV and music talent simply going about their business. Stars from the disparate worlds of TV, film, music and art would often be seen cheek-by-jowel, shopping for baps in Dunns bakery, or politely waiting their turn to use the cubicles in one of the local hostelries, clutching their cocaine wraps to their palms. What a great place! Where else could you see Annie Lennox drunkenly breaking a chair over the back of Placido Domingo after a sambuca binge? Or TV actor John Simm duetting on 'Dead Ringer For Love' with *Loose Women*'s Jane Macdonald?

Mandy delivers on this subject with a litany of great local celebs and the haunts they hang in. She also doesn't fail to hit us with the greatest of all Dylan urban myths. Mind you, if it could happen anywhere, it could happen in Crouche Ende, refuge of the famous.

Playlist

▷ **Eurythmics** – Love Is A Stranger

▷ **The Tourists** – I Only Want To Be With You

FAVOURITE FACTS

- There's an amusing blue plaque on a house in Crouch End which says that Carswell Prentice, who invented the shopping trolley, stayed at that house in 1932. I've since found out that this is a fake blue plaque and the real inventor was someone called Sylvan Goldman, the owner of the Humpty Dumpty Supermarket in Oklahoma City in 1937.

- Nearby at Alexandra Palace I discovered only the other week there is a Cold War nuclear observation bunker – it's covered in brambles and fenced in, but it's there!

- Annie Lennox and Dave Stewart used to drink in a local pub called the Queen's in the seventies before they were famous.

- Dave Stewart opened a studio in a converted church on Crouch Hill. There's a legend which says that Bob Dylan once knocked on what he thought was Dave Stewart's door; the woman who opened the door didn't recognize him and let him wait in the kitchen of this house for 'Dave' to come home. Eventually, when Dave the plumber comes home, he finds Bob Dylan waiting for him!

- *Shaun of the Dead* was filmed around here, and our landlord's grocery shop features in it a couple of times, including the bit where he slips on the blood on the floor without realizing because he's looking at a can he's just got from the fridge. Comedy connections don't stop there: the opening credits to *Peep Show* are filmed near the Town Hall.

LOCAL HEROES

★ Lots of actors live in Crouch End, and our most spotted one is Minty from *EastEnders* - you can almost guarantee to see him at least once a week, in one of the local pubs or restaurants.

★ Other famous faces are Phil Davis, Peter Capaldi and Cathy Tyson.

SIDCUP

TOASTER: STUART ROBINSON

> **Playlist**
>
> ▷ **The Rolling Stones** – Gimme Shelter

FAVOURITE FACTS

- Sidcup was the centre of the 'Dasani' scandal in 2004, when Coca-Cola tried to sell purified Sidcup tap water for 95p a pop.

- Mick Jagger and Keith Richards first agreed to form a band on the platform of Sidcup railway station.

- At the Roundhouse Morrissey introduced himself by saying 'My name is Stanley Ogden, and I come from Sidcup.'

- The MP for Bexley and Sidcup is dodgy Derek Conway, who paid his son to be a researcher whilst at university.

LOCAL HEROES

- ★ Quentin Blake

- ★ John Paul Jones

- ★ Mel C

- ★ Gary Oldman

KENNINGTON

TOASTER: MATT WARNES

> **Playlist**
>
> ▷ **The Stranglers** – Golden Brown (Gordon Brown likes his Kennington curries)

FAVOURITE FACTS

- Kennington is on what was the Roman road from London to Chichester. It was later home to the Black Prince, whilst Chaucer worked there in 1389.

- Kennington Common hosted the second ever international cricket match (1724); it's now home to the Oval cricket ground.

- Some of the most important London marches started in Kennington Park: that of the Chartists in 1848, the first Gay Pride in 1986, the Poll Tax march in 1990 and the Liverpool dockers' march in 1998.

- The first bomb in the First World War was dropped from a Zeppelin onto Kennington Park in 1914.

LOCAL HEROES

★ Paddy Pantsdown drinks in a pub in Kennington.

★ Charles Kennedy almost knocked me off my bike once.

****

* Gordon Brown, Alistair Darling and Jack Straw like to eat at the Kennington curry house 'Ghandis' – apparently Brown still sends a driver there to pick up curries.

* Richard and Judy film all their shows in Kennington.

* Charlie Chaplin spent part of his childhood in Kennington.

* Pierce Brosnan started acting at a theatre in Kennington.

* Sarah Walters, author of *Tipping the Velvet*, lives in Kennington.

ENFIELD

TOASTER: PAUL DENGEL

Playlist

▷ **The Buggles** – Video Killed The Radio Star

FAVOURITE FACTS

➤ The area was once mostly woodland and was very popular with kings and queens for hunting (Elizabeth I and Edward VI were in Enfield, barely a mile from my house, when their father, Henry VIII, died and Edward was made king). It was also a favoured hideout of Dick Turpin, who is said to still haunt the area.

➤ Andy Abraham, the 'Singing Dustman' who represented Britain at the fifty-third Eurovision Song Contest, lived in a former council house at the end of my road until very recently.

****

- Enfield had the world's first cashpoint in 1967, opened by none other than Reg Varney from *On the Buses*. Reg also owned what I believe was the first pizza takeaway in the area.

> **SHAUN SEZ:** It's alleged one of the reasons Suede split up was because of Brett Anderson's relentless use of *On the Buses* catchphrase 'I'll get you Butler' directed at his long-suffering guitarist Bernard Butler.

- The diode valve was apparently invented in Enfield, the device that gave us radio, TV and eventually computers. Enfield was also the place where the first colour TV was made, on a site that's now a Morrison's supermarket.

LOCAL HEROES

★ Reg Varney

★ Benjamin Disraeli

★ Bruce Forsyth

★ Paul McKenna

★ Amy Winehouse

(I also went to the same primary school as Chris Akabusi, but not at the same time.)

STOKE NEWINGTON

TOASTER: RACHEL WRATHALL

Playlist

▷ **Stricken City** – Tak O Tak (the drummer lives here,
where they rehearse together)

FAVOURITE FACTS

➤ According to *Time Out*, Hackney is 'lesbian central [and]
Stoke Newington, on the northern fringes, is possibly the
capital's most Sapphic suburb'.

➤ The former Water Board pumping station was
designed to look like a towering Scottish castle to
keep the complaining locals at bay. It's now a very
good climbing centre.

➤ Like pretty much everywhere else in North London,
we have a farmer's market every weekend. But (not to be
outdone) ours was the first in the UK to have only organic
and biodynamic producers.

LOCAL HEROES

★ Marc Bolan, the lead singer of T Rex, was brought up here.

★ Mark 'Bedders' Bedford, bass player with Madness, lives
here, as does John Power, the bassist from the La's.

★ Tjinder Singh, lead singer of Cornershop, currently lives here.

★ Authors Daniel Defoe, Edgar Allan Poe and Mary
Wollstonecraft lived or were schooled in Stokey.

****

R2D2 LIVES IN PRESTON

ISLINGTON

TOASTER: MATT HALL

FAVOURITE FACTS

- Islington sits on a hill, which used to provide most of the water to the City of London, until the City grew too large in the seventeenth century and the New River was constructed to bring in water from the River Lee.

- Mayor and blond clown extraordinaire Boris Johnson lives here, and when he returns home late at night can be seen running the gauntlet past the drunks outside the York pub.

- The last king of Wales stayed there when on his way to pay a tribute to the king of England, but was so disgusted

****

by the display put on by the Islington locals, he vowed instead to fight the English until his dying breath – which he did. Didn't win of course.

- The Angel Islington is on the Monopoly board (one of the light blues) and is also mentioned in *Jonathan Strange & Mr Norrell* by Susanna Clarke. In Neil Gaiman's *Neverwhere* there is an angel called Islington.

- The Regent's Canal goes into a tunnel as it passes Upper Street. This tunnel is known to be home to trolls and goblins.

LOCAL HEROES

★ Douglas Adams

★ Lily Allen

★ Kathy Burke

★ John Glasscock from Jethro Tull.

★ George Orwell

★ John Foxx from Ultravox.

★ Charlie Watts of The Rolling Stones.

SHOREDITCH

TOASTER: STEVE SCOTT

Playlist

▷ **Ramsey Lewis** – The In Crowd

FAVOURITE FACTS

- The sitcom *Rev* starring Tom Hollander as a vicar had its exterior shots filmed at Shoreditch church, which was designed by sixteenth-century architect Nicholas Hawksmoor, who apparently had ties to the occult.

- We have the Boundary Estate, the first council estate built in England. It's still standing with the original buildings. We also have a bandstand in the centre of the estate. But we have no band. That would make it a shelter then?

- Best of all, we have one of the most diverse communities in all of England.

LOCAL HEROES

★ Our most famous nearby celebrities include Jack the Ripper and Gilbert and George. I've lived here a long time but I didn't know Jack and I've only met the other two twice.

BARKING

TOASTER: CATHRYN

Playlist

▷ **Billy Bragg** – Way Over Yonder In The Minor Key

FAVOURITE FACTS

- I can't help but be amused by the grand-sounding announcement 'This is Barking' when alighting from either train or tube, because it's basically regarded as a grim outpost on the border of London and Essex.

- The Ilford Mammoth was found nearby, and is now on display in the Natural History Museum.

****

- It has a thriving Asian community, which provoked the BBC recently to make a documentary, *It's All White in Barking*, which followed a group of white people getting to know their neighbours, with mostly positive results.

- Captain Cook got married there in 1762.

- Elizabeth Fry (important social reformer, also known as the lady off the £5 notes) is buried next to the Barking Tesco's.

- Billy Bragg is known as the 'Bard of Barking' because he attended Barking Abbey School.

- We've got the lowest adult literacy in the UK.

LOCAL HEROES

★ Dudley Moore

★ Sir Alf Ramsey

★ David Essex

★ Bobby Moore

★ Trevor Brooking

WALTHAMSTOW

TOASTER: OLIVER TOOLEY

Playlist

▷ **Led Zeppelin** – Whole Lotta Love (Led Zeppelin
never played here, so instead I'm going to finally
get them to play a song)

FAVOURITE FACTS

➥ We have a strong musical heritage. The boy band E17
were born and raised in E17 but no sooner did they make
a few quid than they moved to E4.

➥ The well-wicked hoodie gangsta rappers Blazing Squad
were from Chingford. I met them a few times and they are
actually a very well-behaved bunch of middle-class kids!

➥ Sir Winston Churchill's coach was turned over on the
high street in rioting during the General Strike of 1926.

LOCAL HEROES

★ William Morris, nineteenth-century designer
and philosopher.

★ Keith Albarn, manager of Soft Machine and father
of Damon, taught here in the 1960s.

★ Ian Dury studied here too.

★ Phil Collen of Def Leppard.

★ Clement Attlee

****

BURY ST EDMUNDS

'THE PERFECT PLACE
TO BRING AN ORGANISED GROUP'
visit-burystedmunds.co.uk

Witchfinder General. What a grand job description that is. I somehow imagine that the Witchfinder General would have his own office (naturally with 'Witchfinder General' etched in the glass of the door), defer lesser witchfinding duties to his underling, the Witchfinder Colonel, have long boozy lunches in town with other witchfinders of similar rank and harbour daydreams that one day he might make it to the front cover of *Which Witchfinder General* magazine.

Sadly this is all nothing more than my own fevered imaginings. In fact witchfinding, burning and/or drowning was a very dark and ignominious epsiode of our British history, a ghost briefly resurrected by Toaster Steve, who reminds us that his hometown, as well as being famous for Lovejoy, sugar and the invention of the internally illuminated sign, was also the Old Bailey of its day for witch litigation. As we all know, any suspected witch back in those dank, medieval times would be tied to a ducking stool and drowned. If she sank she was innocent, if she floated she was guilty. Luckily, such treatment of witches is no longer tolerated. Though it is for football managers.

TOASTER: STEVE HOLDEN

(a.k.a. regular listener Grumpy Steve. I hope this temporarily makes you less grumpy!)

Playlist

▷ **Mansun** – Wide Open Space (Mansun played locally at the Carnegie back in about 1998)

▷ **The Undertones** – Here Comes The Summer (because of the John Peel connection)

FAVOURITE FACTS

- Bury St Edmunds was the setting for two witch trials. The first was under the direction of the Witchfinder General and the second was used as a reference in the Salem Witch Trials of 1692 and 1693.

- Near the gardens stands Britain's first internally illuminated street sign, known as the Pillar of Salt. When it was built it needed permission because it did not conform to regulations.

- Bury Town FC is the fourth oldest non-League team in England. They are members of the Southern Football League Division One Midlands (which looks like it needs a colon or something in it, but doesn't have one).

- Bury's largest landmark is the British Sugar factory near the A14, which processes sugar beet into refined crystal sugar. It was built in 1925, processes beet from 1,300 growers and stinks to high heaven!

****

- Bury has the UK's largest British-owned brewery, Greene King, as well as Britain's smallest public house, the Nutshell.

- Legend John Peel lived in nearby Great Finborough and, on 12 November 2004, his funeral took place at Bury Cathedral. It was attended by approximately a thousand people, including many artists he had championed, and all sang along to 'Teenage Kicks' by The Undertones when it was played into the streets.

> **SHAUN SEZ**: RIP, John, one of the great broadcasters who inspired me, yet I was destined never to meet.

LOCAL HEROES

★ Bob Hoskins

★ John Le Mesurier grew up in the town.

★ Ian McShane was given the freedom of the borough in 1996 for his role in the television series *Lovejoy*, which was filmed in and around Bury.

★ Bands: Miss Black America, The Dawn Parade, Jacob's Mouse, Kate Jackson of the sadly defunct Long Blondes.

FROME

Look, as far as I'm concerned, life is complex enough without *deliberately* screwing around with stuff. It was bad enough when Walkers crisps changed the colour-coding of snack flavours in the eighties. Until those dickheads came along, EVERYONE knew that salt and vinegar = light blue packet, ready salted = dark blue packet, and cheese and onion were yellow/green packet. OUT OF THE LEFT FIELD one day, these feckless manufacturers, with little or no care for the consequences to children everywhere, changed the whole playing field!

It the same with pronunciations (is that pronounced proNUNciation or proNOUNciation?) For example, why does Ralph Fiennes insist that his name is pronounced Raiffe? Don't choose a name with a spelling that will definitely make people think your name is pronounced one way, and then get *annoyed* when they get it wrong, OK? The same level of ire is directed at the foolish yet picturesque setting of Frome, sorry FrOOOme, in Somerset. For obvious reasons. Why couldn't the town namers just . . . SLIP ANOTHER 'O' IN THE SPELLING OF THE NAME! THUS AVOIDING MILLIONS OF EMBARRASSING CONVERSATIONS, MISTAKES AND CORRECTIONS! WHAT WERE THEY TRYING TO DO? SAVE MONEY ON INK?!

(NB. I apologize for the vitriol on this page, and for all the CAPITALS. It could be lack of sleep or a slight hangover.)

****

TOASTER: NICK BLOXHAM

> **Playlist**
>
> ▷ **Bob Dylan** – Like A Rolling Stone (it sums up Frome perfectly, sitting in the Griffin with friends, with great beer, listening to the band covering this. A perfect Friday night!)

FAVOURITE FACTS

- Frome is an old market town in East Somerset. For quite a small place, it has a good annual Frome Festival. Paul Merton headlined last year and Van Morrison played a couple of years back.

- The last band I saw in Frome was Phantom Limb, who played at the legendary Griffin pub.

- Frome's Cheap Street was used as a location in *The Fall and Rise of Reginald Perrin*.

LOCAL HEROES

★ Jenson Button

SHAUN SEZ: What is it about Formula 1 racing drivers I can't stand? Oh YEAH, I remember! It's the untold millions in the bank, the houses in Mustique, Monte Carlo and Chelsea, the yachts, the underwear models and the job smashing a plane-powered car around a racetrack. YES, it's true — envy is a terrible and destructive thing. Mind you, at least I don't have the name Jenson Button. That's a bobbins name, that is.

★ Pee Wee Ellis, who used to be James Brown's saxophonist, lives there.

★ Lois Maxwell (Miss Moneypenny) lived here for a while.

EXETER

As a kid, my main obsessions (notwithstanding fruit and veg avoidance) were swimming baths, hide and seek, walkie-talkies and underground tunnels. Which is why I was particularly interested in Toaster David Myers' Exeter entry, and his fact about 'tunnels under the city'. As an unusually fatalistic child, I was dogged by the fear of imminent nuclear holocaust, and constantly considered my options for survival should the Ruskies drop a red warhead on the Leigh/Wigan area (they'd need to take the nation's primary pie-production site out first to destroy our morale, I reasoned). I later saw a programme about London's secret tunnels, and was disappointed to learn that they had been constructed specifically for the use and protection of Heads of State and the Prime Minister. 'What a cow!' I thought about Thatch. 'She's nicked my school milk, now she's robbing me of my only chance of survival in the event of atomic immolation!' I never really forgave her after that, and felt sure she instinctively knew that she had lost my vote, were I old enough to cast one.

While we're at it, let's all remember the good times with walkie-talkies! What witchcraft it was back in the early eighties to walk round the cul-de-sac with your best mate with a cheap pair of Police-issue Hasbro Walkie-Talkies! The conversation almost always went like this:

SHAUN: KKKKHHHHHH – KHHHHHH – KH – KH –
BAAAAAAAAAH . . .
FRIEND 1: KHH . . . BB-B-B—EEEEEEEEE . . .
SHAUN: (*shouting over the wall directly at Friend 1*) DID

****

YOU HEAR ANY OF THAT?
FRIEND 1: (*also shouting*) NO! I THINK WE NEED TO CHANGE THE BATTERIES!

Great days! Even as an adult, they're far more exciting than mobile phones. The fact that I can call literally anyone, anywhere in the world, on this 4-inch piece of plastic in my top pocket means LESS THAN NOTHING to me. But stand me next to a security guard with a crackly walkie-talkie, and I am restraining every instinct within me to shout, 'Let me have a go, *pleeeeze*!'

TOASTERS: VERITY GROOM
DAVID MYERS

Playlist

▷ **Muse** – Plug In Baby, or Starlight (Muse are officially from Teignmouth, which is 10 miles from Exeter, but they lived and played in Exeter in their formative years)

FAVOURITE FACTS

← Exeter is the county city of Devon. It has a big cathedral and there are medieval tunnels that run beneath the city.

← It was at one time the most south-westerly settlement of the Roman Empire in Britain, when it was known as Isca.

← Exeter City were the first ever team to play the national side of Brazil at football, in 1914.

****

- In 2002 Michael Jackson and Uri Geller were made honorary directors of Exeter City FC. Ade Edmonson is also a season ticket holder.

> **SHAUN SEZ:** Little known fact about the spoonbender Uri. He once worked in a branch of Ryman's Stationers but was sacked for bending the rules. (Tumbleweed)

- We have a great guitar shop – called Mansons – who have made guitars for Muse, Oasis, The Arctic Monkeys and Led Zeppelin!

LOCAL HEROES

★ Chris Martin was born here, and Coldplay played their first gigs at Exeter's club The Cavern.

★ Tommy Cooper lived here for a while.

★ Past students from Exeter University include Thom Yorke, whose band at the time was The Headless Chickens, Will Young, Felix Buxton (one half of Basement Jaxx) and J. K. Rowling, the twelfth-richest woman in Britain.

WEYMOUTH

Here's a Trivial Pursuit question for you. Where were many of the questions for the Trivial Pursuit board game researched? That's RIGHT, it *was* the Weymouth Public Library! How the hell did you know that? Oh, you read it on this page? Fairdoos. Thanks to Toaster Matt Bath for his contribution to our book, and also for the fact that *a foreign ship docking at Weymouth is believed to have brought the Black Death into Britain in 1348*. Wow. That's heavy, isn't it? I mean, we all make mistakes, but that's a biggie. I for one have definitely gone out to the pub and left the grill on *numerous* times in the past, THANKFULLY without causing a major fire. I know many of us will have entered a shared property under the influence of alcohol and left the main front door swinging open, in full sight of local robbers and ne'er-do-wells. There was that time as a primary school pupil when I forgot to feed the class goldfish, Starsky and Hutch, thus causing their no doubt harrowing and needless deaths. But none of that comes *close* to accidentally bringing the BLACK DEATH TO BRITAIN!

My producer, Nic, has some idea of how that Skipper of Death must have felt like, as he infected me and some other members of the breakfast team with bubonic plague back in 2009. Luckily for us all it turned out to be a case of the slightly less deadly man-flu.

NB. Re: Lassie fact. I have it on good authority that, despite Lassie's on-screen good nature and willingness to help anyone in trouble, she was in real life a right nasty piece of work. She bit seven co-stars, was involved in a dog-fighting ring and had no fewer than seventeen pups with five different fathers. AND ONE WAS HER BROTHER! Filthy bitch.

TOASTER: MATT BATH

Playlist

Feeder – Buck Rodgers (because I drink cider from eleven)

FAVOURITE FACTS

- A foreign ship docking at Weymouth is believed to have brought the Black Death into Britain in 1348.

- Many of the questions for the original Trivial Pursuit game were researched in the public library in Weymouth.

****

- 2012 Olympics sailing events are to be held in Weymouth bay. (Local sailors Sarah Ayton and Nick Dempsey are Olympic medallists.)

- There is a local tradition to swim the harbour on Christmas Day.

- There are about thirty-seven pubs in half a square mile. It's said to be in the top ten places to go out in the UK on New Year's Eve. Everyone dresses up, and I mean *everyone*. The best pub in Weymouth is the Boot Inn, dating from the seventeeth century and reputed to be both the oldest and the most haunted inn in Weymouth.

- We have the worst ever Elvis impersonator in the world. Called Jumping Jimmy Thunder, he looks nothing like Elvis and sings out of key most if not all of the time and wears a costume made by his mum.

- We have the biggest seagulls in the world. They have been known to swoop down and snatch small children.

LOCAL HEROES

★ Lassie, the collie dog made famous by a series of Hollywood movies, apparently hailed from Weymouth.

MIDHURST

Poor old Guy Fawkes. I mean, OK, he *did* almost blow up the Houses of Parliament, but really, children burning effigies of him every 5th November for centuries after his death? Is that not something of an overreaction?

Toaster Steve has a nice Fawkes fact in his toast below. It made me think of a business idea I recently had. What with the recent resurgence of fundamentalist belief systems in this and other countries, I feel there is a gap in the market for someone to make money as a professional effigy manufacturer. Let's face facts, the ones you see on the news are rubbish. Imagine if you started a company that created bespoke lifelike effigies of anyone from Osama Bin Laden and Rupert Murdoch to Emma Bunton? A killing could be made.

I love Steve's other nugget about one of Prince Charles's bodyguards standing on his neighbour's toe – that's quintessentially TTN. He also claims that Prince Charles met Queen of our Hearts and People's Princess Lady Di at a polo ground in the town. I guess there are only certain types of places royals meet their future spouses. Here is a top five of places royals have, to date, never met their future spouses:

1 Nando's
2 A Wetherspoon's
3 Night bus
4 Kebab shop queue
5 Chicago Rock Café

****

TOASTER: STEVE PURVES

Playlist

▷ **Pink Floyd** – Crazy Diamond

FAVOURITE FACTS

- Midhurst is a market town situated on the River Rother and is home to the magnificent ruin of the Tudor Cowdray House and the stately Victorian Cowdray Park. *Country Life* magazine once rated Midhurst the second-best town in England.

- Guy Fawkes was once employed at the local castle, now Cowdray Ruins. In 1605 its owner, Anthony Maria-Browne, was arrested in connection with the Gunpowder Plot.

- It is reported that Prince Charles (a regular visitor) met Lady Diana Spencer at the local polo ground – although at least one other polo ground makes the same claim. Also, one of his bodyguards did once tread on one of my neighbour's toes.

LOCAL HEROES

★ H. G. Wells, author of *War of the Worlds*, was a pupil at Midhurst Grammar School.

★ None other than Mr (3-2-1) Ted Rogers is also (or was) a regular visitor to Ricos café in Midhurst.

RUISLIP

Playlist

▷ **Cliff Richard** – The Young Ones

FAVOURITE FACTS

- Ruislip translates as 'the wet place where the rushes grow'.

- In 1974 Leslie Thomas wrote a satire on suburbia called *Tropic of Ruislip*; the book's still in print.

- The most famous thing we have is Ruislip Lido – it was used for the World Water Skiing Championships many years ago (you wouldn't dare swim in it now). The classic *Titanic* film *A Night to Remember* and Cliff Richard's *The Young Ones* were filmed here too.

- NOTHING happens here!

LOCAL HEROES

★ The only famous people you're likely to bump into on the high street are Nikki from *Big Brother* or Brandon Block.

WOKINGHAM

Alf of Wokingham's Toast contains one of the best TTN facts of all time. The fact? That none other than leader of the 'free world', US President and 'Sexiest World Leader 2008/2009' award-winner Barack Obama, went on a stag do in this leafy Berkshire town in 1996! How amazing is that?!

Don't get me wrong, the sense of achievement and pride that comes of becoming the first ever black President of the United States must be a source of constant happiness for Obama, but I am betting there are moments, during high-pressure talks with Middle Eastern counterparts or in the midst of Senate bill wrangles, that he closes his eyes and thinks of simpler times. Of black sambuca shots, two-for-one Smirnoff Ice deals and lascivious Berkshire housewives grabbing his ass. Let's face it, he might be able to reform the American healthcare system and repair international relations, but one thing he definitely *cannot* do is be seen vomiting into a plant pot in an All Bar One straddled by a St Trinian's-themed stripper. No. That's how Bill Clinton would have finished the night.

A personal Wokingham Memory: my mates Al, Dom, Leon and I once jumped the ticket barriers at Wokingham train station to avoid the £4 fare, thus leaving us an extra two pints' worth each of beer money. Since that day I have been a fugitive from the law, constantly looking over my shoulder, certain I will one day be brought to justice for the crime. Kids, please, I implore you, don't EVER evade train fares. My life has been ruined by the guilt and lies.

****

TOASTER: ALF GARNETT

(real name is Jeffrey, which only his mother calls him!)

Playlist

▷ **Doves** – Pounding (because of our bell foundry, tenuous but one of my fave songs)

FAVOURITE FACTS

- Barack Obama came to Wokingham in 1996 for a stag do. They ended up in the Three Frogs pub, where a strippergram appeared. He promptly made his excuses and left.

- In 2007 Wokingham was voted the best place to live in the UK.

- Was once upon a time popular for its bull baiting, which stopped in 1821. At one time it was also well known for its bell foundry.

> **SHAUN SEZ:** There is still an appetite for bull baiting. But due to it being outlawed, modern bull baiters use other techniques to bait the bulls, such as whispering insults, flicking peanuts and singing deliberately off-key.

- 1971 British horror flick *Blind Terror* starring Mia Farrow was shot entirely in Wokingham.

LOCAL HEROES

★ Alexander Pope, poet.

★ The Cooper Temple Clause

★ Nicholas Hoult, actor (*About a Boy*, *Skins*).

★ Will Young

★ Claude Duval, French highwayman.

★ Dick Francis – his dad owned the blacksmith's in the town.

ROMFORD

TOASTER: STEVEN DAVIES

Playlist

▷ **Ian Dury** – Razzle In My Pocket

FAVOURITE FACTS

- Romford Market has been trading since 1247, and is one of the oldest markets in the south-east. It also has the second-oldest pub in Essex, the Golden Lion, which has stood on Market Place since the early 1400s.

- It is the home of the fictional hospital Darkplace, which featured in spoof comedy *Garth Marenghi's Darkplace*.

- Underworld refer to the town in their nineties hit 'Born Slippy', singing 'True blonde going back to Romford, Mega mega, Going back to Romford'.

- Ian Dury, raised nearby, tells his tale of stealing a pornographic magazine from a shop on South Street, Romford, in 'Razzle In My Pocket'.

LOCAL HEROES

★ Ian Dury

BRIGHTON

TOASTERS: MIKE GREEN
HELEN BUCKLEY-HOFFMAN
DONNA LONSDALE O'BRIEN

Playlist

▷ **The Levellers** – One Way

▷ **Curtis Mayfield** – Move On Up

▷ **Devon Sproule** – Stop By

▷ **Midfield General** – Disco Sirens (he's from Brighton)

▷ **Marlene Shaw** – Wade In The Water

▷ **The Who** – The Real Me (opening track in *Quadrophenia*)

▷ **The Jam** – That's Entertainment

FAVOURITE FACTS

- Brighton was burned to the ground by French raiders in 1514.

- It was originally made famous by the Prince Regent in the early 1800s when he started coming down for weekends. It then became known in later years as the place to come for 'dirty' weekends. In a national poll it was also recently voted one of Britain's happiest cities!

- Abba won the 1974 Eurovision performing at the Brighton Dome.

****

- Brighton has a Beard and Moustache Championship every year! As well as one of Britain's first nudist beaches.

LOCAL HEROES

★ The Levellers and The Kooks.

★ Nick Cave now lives in Hove, Brighton.

★ Fatboy Slim + Zoë Ball.

★ Des Lynam

★ Chris Eubank

★ British Sea Power, band famous for *Waving Flags.*

★ Kevin Rowland, front man for Dexy's Midnight Runners.

★ Will Young moved here recently.

SOUTHAMPTON

We've all been there. You're in a pub, after a few scoops, and some lairy pillock *always* ends up asking the same question: 'EYY! SHAUN! DID THE PILGRIM FATHERS SET SAIL FOR AMERICA FROM SOUTHAMPTON OR PLYMOUTH?!' Well, let me try to square this one up. Sally's Toast below states correctly that the Pilgrim Fathers set sail from Southampton Docks in 1620 for America, but a previous Toaster also makes this historical claim for Plymouth. How could this be? Well, it seems they're both right. The Pilgrim Fathers (or the P-Daddies as I will refer to them from now on) did set sail originally from Plymouth, but had to set down almost immediately in Southampton for repairs before their groundbreaking journey to the New World. During their pitstop they loaded up with Ginsters pasties, travel sweets and copies of *Scurvy and Rickets Monthly* magazine in readiness for the lengthy Atlantic crossing.

Good on Sally for also reminding us of the lasting legacy of van manufacture we have her fair city to thank for. Southampton has been producing the Ford Transit for over forty years, and assembled its five millionth in 2005. Without their stellar engineering work, think of the millions of sofas that would have gone unmoved, and the countless attractive young ladies who would not have been lasciviously wolf-whistled at.

TOASTER: SALLY WESTLEY

FAVOURITE FACTS

- The Pilgrim Fathers departed from Southampton in August 1620 on their way to the New World.

- Southampton has the oldest bowling green, dating from before 1299, and it's still in use. A competition takes place on it every August for the Knighthood of the Old Green – the winner is afterwards entitled to be called Sir within the club but is banned from future competitions.

- Southampton is the home of the Spitfire, the Transit Van and B&Q.

- The enormous IKEA which opened in February 2009 can be viewed from every angle of the city!

LOCAL HEROES

★ Sir Isaac Watts, hymn writer – 'O God Our Help In Ages Past' (which plays every four hours from the Civic Centre clock).

★ Will Champion from Coldplay.

★ Craig David

★ King Canute – according to legend, Canute commanded the tide to halt, but the tide refused to stop. He then leaped backwards and said, 'Let all men know how empty and worthless is the power of kings, for there is none worthy of the name, but He whom heaven, earth, and sea obey by eternal laws.' It might make him sound like a bit of a pillock, but apparently he did it to show his scheming courtiers that they couldn't persuade him he had godlike powers. This apparently happened in Southampton, but it is commemorated by a plaque in Bosham in West Sussex as well.

★ Benny Hill

> **SHAUN SEZ:** The weirdest thing happened in our house recently. My young son Arthur pressed the preset button on his electric keyboard, and what should come out but the Benny Hill theme! And what was weirder was that, immediately upon hearing this, Arthur started to run around the room in circles giggling. TRUE FACT! It seems that the tune is designed specifically to cause people to run around in fast circles.

LEWES

TOASTER: SIMON RUCKES

Playlist

▷ **Catherine Wheel** – Black Mechanic

▷ **The Smiths** – William It Was Really Nothing

▷ **Sham 69** – Borstal Breakout

FAVOURITE FACTS

➤ Lewes has the grandest bonfire night celebrations in the country. There are seven bonfire societies who each put on their own bonfire and fireworks display around the town and burn huge topical effigies.

- In 1768 Thomas Paine, a radical propagandist and voice of the common man, arrived in Lewes from London. In 1787 he penned his most influential work, *The Rights of Man*. In it he attacked hereditary government and recommended family allowances, old age pensions and maternity grants. The pamphlet was banned and he was charged with libel.

- When Lewes football club's popular manager, Steven King, guided them into the Conference National for the first time in the 2007–8 season he controversially did not have his contract renewed, and all but one of the players in the squad left the club. The next season they came last and were demoted again.

- Lewes has a holding prison. A few years back a mate of mine got on the roof during a riot. When asked what his demands were he replied: 'A helicopter, one million pounds and a KFC bucket.'

PLYMOUTH

TOASTER: ANDREW COTTER

Playlist

▷ **The Breeders** – Cannonball (ties in with Drake defeating the Spanish)

▷ **The Go! Team** – Ladyflash (as a lighthouse beacon flashes)

FAVOURITE FACTS

- We've got the Mayflower Steps, where the Pilgrim Fathers set sail from on their voyage to America.

- Sir Francis Drake famously played bowls on Plymouth Hoe before taking on and defeating the Spanish Armada.

- Situated on the Hoe is Smeaton's Tower, a landmark which used to be a lighthouse out in the English Channel. There is a photograph of The Beatles when they stopped off in the city on the way to France. They're relaxing on the Hoe with Smeaton's Tower on their left as they look out to sea.

- Plymouth is the largest city not to have had a football team in the top flight (a dubious honour we used to share with Hull until their promotion in 2008).

LOCAL HEROES

★ Sir Francis Drake

★ Wayne Sleep

★ Beryl Cook, the artist.

★ Sharon Davies, Olympic swimmer.

★ Tom Daley, the young diver who appeared in the Beijing Olympics in 2008.

BOURNEMOUTH

'Oh how the poorest and the richest liveth cheek by jowl in this, our nation drunk on democracy!' Who is this quote attributed to? Homer? Descartes? Wilde? Nah. Of course I made it up. Seems to me, all you have to do to make a quote look right is stick it in italics, and antiquate it up by sticking an 'Oh!' at the front or perhaps a 'liveth' every now and again . . .

Nonetheless. Despite its lack of authentic provenance, the basic point is true. Rich and poor really DO live cheek by jowl. This point has never been so well illustrated as by my Toaster Leah from Bournemouth, who reveals her place of birth to be one of great fiscal extremes. Not only does it count among its districts Sandbanks, one of the most sought-after property areas in Europe, but it's also called home by an entertaining homeless man known simply as Gordon the Tramp, who can tell the exact time despite not owning a timepiece. Leah's song choice, Supertramp's 'The Logical Song', initially chosen as original member Richard Palmer comes from Bournemouth, takes on a whole new level of resonance in this instance.

I also like the fact page three girl Lucy Pinder was 'discovered' on Bournemouth beach. She was discovered, not as was initially presumed, by the *Financial Times*, but by the *Daily Star*. I'm not sure how they make these discoveries, but I *imagine* they have a converted ice cream van with a periscope protruding from the top, with the words BOOB PATROL signwritten on the sides, with the double Os made to look like ladies' breasts. Upon spotting some page three talent, the theme tune to

Benny Hill commences, and the chase across the beach in x6 motion begins.

(I must stress, that is only how I *imagine* the *Daily Star* spot page three talent. The reality may be more mundane.)

TOASTER: LEAH STEVENS

Playlist

▷ **Supertramp** – The Logical Song (Richard Palmer, one of the original members of Supertramp, was from Bournemouth)

▷ **Coldplay** – Yellow (the obvious choice)

▷ **Dead Kennedys** – Funland At The Beach

FAVOURITE FACTS

- Bournemouth was voted the happiest place to live in the UK in 2008.

- The video for Coldplay's 'Yellow' was filmed on the famous Studland beach, which isn't really Bournemouth, but it's near enough.

- The IMAX cinema on Bournemouth sea front was recently voted one of the UK's top ten ugliest buildings.

- Once, before a gig, Roy Stride from Scouting For Girls had to jump into the sea to rescue his dog because it didn't know how to swim.

****

LOCAL HEROES

★ Harry Redknapp

★ Max Bygraves

★ Geoff Boycott

★ Murray Walker, honorarily educated at Bournemouth Uni.

★ Both Jamie and Harry Redknapp live on the Sandbanks peninsula, which is the fourth-most expensive place in the world to live (by area).

★ Alex James from Blur was born here.

★ Steve Lamacq was born here too.

★ Lucy Pinder was 'discovered' on Bournemouth beach.

★ The most famous person in Bournemouth is Gordon the Tramp, who is known all over the UK for being able to tell you the exact time even though he never wears a watch!

LINTON

It's wonderful to see so many pubs mentioned in Toast the Nation entries. To me this is proof-positive that, despite continued embattlement of the pub industry from many fronts, they are still as dear to many peoples' hearts as they always were. Toaster Dave the chemist names his three locals in the town of Linton, and they're all pretty traditionally named. I have myself, however, recently noticed that pub names are getting sillier. One recently opened near me called the Cock and Bottle. Now what *possible* business does a cock have with a bottle? Of course I am innocently presuming that the cock in question is of the feathered variety. A nurse friend who worked in A and E at Wigan General did once tell me a story about a cock and bottle, the dénouement of which would certainly *not* look nice on one of those painted swinging pub signs.

Other ridiculous pub names that have recently come to my attention include:

1 The Spaniel and Hermaphrodite
2 The Fair-minded Estate Agent
3 Camel Camel Camel
4 The Turtle's Head
5 The Queen's Head in a Bag

TOASTER: DAVE CHEMIST

Playlist

▷ **MGMT** – Kids

▷ **The Howling Bells** – Setting Sun

▷ **Mansun** – Wide Open Space

▷ **The Scorpions** – Wind of Change

FAVOURITE FACTS

- Linton is a village 10 miles south of Cambridge on the border of three counties: Cambridgshire, Suffolk and Essex.

- It has three pubs: the Wagon and Horses, the Dog and Duck and the Crown, although the Wagon is a little unfriendly.

- It has a couple of local landmarks: Chilford Hall, which produces wine, and Rivey water tower, which I am reliably informed is an example of Art Deco.

LOCAL HERO

★ Linton's most famous patron is probably Alan Partridge, who stayed at the Linton Travel Tavern because of its favourable location, being equidistant between London and Norwich...

****

CATFORD

'CATFORD HAS PLENTY TO KEEP YOU AMUSED'
catford.towntalk.co.uk

TOASTER: KAMEIL SATTAR

Playlist

▷ **Cat Stevens** – Peace Train

FAVOURITE FACTS

- Catford gained its name from the big cats that used to cross the Rivers Ravensbourne in Saxon times.

- Catford lays claim to the first curry house, dating back to *1824*. [A cursory internet search shows this not to be true. Sorry. The Hindoostane Curry House in Piccadilly opened in 1810, and that wasn't necessarily the first one. Ed.]

- There are no hotels in Catford.

- Boasts one of the highest rates for teenage pregnancies in Europe.

LOCAL HEROES

★ Tommy Steele was a resident in the late fifties.

★ Ben Elton

★ Nick Hancock has been spotted on the high street.

****

★ Cat Stevens lived above a furniture store in Catford in the sixties.

SHAUN SEZ: Heh! Cat Stevens living in CATford. Heh! Get it?

★ Shoe bomber Richard Reid lived in a hostel in Catford.

★ Sir Henry Cooper

OXFORD

Where I live in London (ripped from the heart and hearth of my northern brethren to toil for up to four hours a day, crouched sweating over an expensive laptop with only herbal teas and pornography for company) postcode snobbery is rife. On every street corner, egregious estate agents in too much cologne proclaim the latest up-and-coming (i.e. currently deadly) area to be *the next big investment opportunity!* Mind you it's true that, although there were full-scale race riots in Notting Hill only twenty-five years ago, the only race riot you'd see there now would involve over-zealous and competitive parents at the St Swithin's Private School Sports Day.

The people of Oxford, though, are so sick of being seen by the rest of the UK as a bunch of bike-riding, mortar-board-doffing, cape-donning, don-spotting, punt-hiring, boater-boasting toffs that they like very much to talk *down* their town. Witness exhibit one here, our Toaster, Paula, who in her first breath hits us with the Ken Loach-ian fact that *Oxford ranks in the lower half of deprived areas, with very high rates of poverty.* BOOF! They never showed you too many hoodie ne'er-do-wells hanging in the stairwells on *Inspector Morse*, did they? 'Lewis! Someone's scraped the words POSH COCK on the jag's door again!'

I also love the personal touch of Paula's here: 'Dudley Moore got a music degree from here, and I stood next to him in a queue once.' In a similar way, I once stood behind Terry Christian in a queue in HMV in Manchester. More gripping stories like this will go to form my three-volume autobiography.

****

Playlist

▷ **Vampire Weekend** – Oxford Comma

▷ **Radiohead** – Jigsaw Falling Into Place

SHAUN SEZ: I have never completed a jigsaw. FACT.

FAVOURITE FACTS

➥ There is a statue of an ox opposite Oxford station where it is customary for people to place an empty takeaway drinks carton so it looks as if the ox is going to wee in it.

➥ Oxford is often depicted as an area of great privilege and educational achievements and, whilst there are areas that are nice, overall Oxford ranks in the lower half of deprived areas, with very high rates of poverty, housing problems and ironically extremely high levels of skill shortages.

➥ Oxford is full of places with fanciful names, such as Jericho, Mesopotamia, Folly Bridge and Music Meadow – as well as South Park, although I have never spotted Stan, Kyle, Kenny or Cartman there.

➥ The new Mini is produced at BMW in Oxford.

➥ We've got Europe's oldest live music venue – the Holywell Music Room, built in 1748.

****

- Oxford's architecture is still with us partly because Hitler was planning to use Oxford as his capital had he succeeded in invading the country and so he did not bomb it.

- The Pitt Rivers Museum has a collection that includes various human remains, including the famous shrunken heads.

LOCAL HEROES

★ Inspector Morse + Lewis

★ Oxford has been home to more published writers per square inch than any other city in the world, including J. R. R. Tolkein, C. S. Lewis and Phillip Pullman, to name a few.

★ James Bond studied Danish at Oxford in *Tomorrow Never Dies*.

★ Radiohead, Supergrass and the Foals hail from here. Thom Yorke from Radiohead can sometimes be spotted eating at the macrobiotic takeaway in the covered market (opposite the butcher's).

* Dudley Moore got a music degree from here, and I stood next to him in a queue once.

* The Chuckle Brothers were born in Oxford, then moved up north when they were babies.

* The Morris Minor car is not strictly a person but has such personality that it should count on this list: it was originally produced at Cowley in Oxford.

* Sir Richard Doll was one of the team of researchers at Oxford University who first found that smoking caused lung cancer.

* Margaret Thatcher, like many of our politicians, studied at Oxford.

SAFFRON WALDEN

TOASTER: WILL HARTLEY

Playlist

▷ **Pink Floyd** – Another Brick In The 'Walden'

▷ **Color Me Badd** – I Want To 'Essex' You Up

FAVOURITE FACTS

- Saffron Walden has possibly the oldest turf maze on record, first referenced in 1699! It also happens to be one of the largest in England, at a mile long. For that reason alone, Saffron Walden is worth a visit. What is a turf maze, you ask? Why, a series of concentric bumps laid out in turf mounds about six inches high...

- Saffron Walden is referenced by Lawrence Durrell in his novel *Balthazar* (1958) as a piece of (almost Cockney) slang. It is explained as a code phrase for 'male brothel', e.g. 'He was caught in a Saffron Walden, old man, covered in jam.'

- In the medieval period the primary trade in the area was in wool. However, in the sixteenth and seventeenth centuries the saffron crocus became widely grown in the area. The flower was precious, as extract from the stigmas was used in medicines, as a condiment, as a perfume, as an aphrodisiac and as an expensive

****

yellow dye. This industry gave its name to the town, and Chipping Walden became Saffron Walden.

LOCAL HEROES

★ Stan Stammers of post-punk bands Theatre Of Hate and Spear Of Destiny fame grew up here.

★ Stephen McGann, one of the lesser-known McGann brothers (as in Paul McGann), was born here. I think he is still an actor.

★ Charles Dunstone, billionaire and the CEO of the Carphone Warehouse, was born here in 1964.

★ My girlfriend used to hang out with Jamie Oliver on the common here when they were growing up.

PETERBOROUGH

Despite being what a Christian fundamentalist would describe as a heretic, an unbeliever or a 'godless, soulless wretch', I dig churches. Places of worship really chill me out. Not those hideous seventies-concocted cocoons of concrete thrown up in a lunchtime, I'm talking about those ancient, mystical monuments to worship that have been standing for centuries. It feels like a sacred privilege to sit among the pews, in the very same place that has seen the vertiginous extremes of life, marriage, baptism and death. It's as if you are cohabiting temporarily with the spirits of all the many people down the ages that have ever experienced a life-changing moment in that very place. That being the case, I am increasingly dismayed to find that such places of historical and religious significance are being converted into O Neill's pubs and Zizzi restaurants. I can just imagine the commemorative stained-glass window a millennium from now in just such an establishment, depicting the 'Battle of Darren's Stolen Mobile' and a commemorative plaque where the toilets once were reading 'Here lies the virginity of Vicky Pemberton'.

Luckily no such fate has befallen the delightful Peterborough Cathedral, which still rises with glorious majesty above the town. Speaking of ale, though, it's nice to know that they have an annual CAMRA beerfest here in Peterborough. I have been to many such an event and can personally vouch for the pasty stalls and the tribute acts. These bands go down brilliantly, however poor they are. This is mostly due to the fact that after seven or eight pints of Scruttocks Bumflaps, the audience are so gloriously battered they think they actually *are* watching The Doors.

TOASTER: YVONNE PUPLETT

Playlist

▷ **The Prodigy** – Out Of Space

▷ **Erasure** – A Little Respect

FAVOURITE FACTS

- The area around Peterborough has been a human settlement since before the Bronze Age.

- The most beautiful thing in Peterborough is the cathedral in the city centre (built 1118–1238). Katherine of Aragon and Mary Queen of Scots were both buried there at one time.

- The great annual event is the CAMRA beer festival every August. It involves lots of beer, cider and, usually, mud. Lots of good live music and tribute acts too on the Friday/Saturday night.

****

LOCAL HEROES

★ Keith Palmer (Maxim Reality) and Gizz Butt from
The Prodigy.

> **SHAUN SEZ:** What on earth possessed Keith to
> change his name to Maxim Reality? What's
> wrong with Keith Palmer if you're going
> to be an MC and frontman for a crossover
> dance act? And how bad must Gizz Butt's
> real name have been for him to want to
> change it TO Gizz Butt? Apparently it was
> Graham.

★ Martin 'Wolfy' Adams, the 2007 Lakeside World
Darts Champion.

★ Andy Bell from Erasure.

★ Louis Smith, who in 2008 became first British gymnast
to win an individual Olympic medal.

LETCHWORTH GARDEN CITY

TOASTER: TABITHA WILSON

Playlist

▷ **Shamen** – Ebeneezer Goode

FAVOURITE FACTS

➤ Letchworth was the world's first official Garden City 1903. That means it was *before* Welwyn Garden City, I have to point out.

➤ Fetchingly, Letchworth Garden City is home to one of the UK's largest colonies of 'black squirrels'.

- Not only that, it's also home to the UK's first roundabout, from *c.* 1909.

- It's the only place in Britain where citizens need two planning applications to do pretty much anything (even for garden hedge and tree removal).

- There were no public houses here until the 1960s. And, ARRRGH, there are only a handful now!

- Everyone here has a funny walk.

LOCAL HEROES

★ Laurence Olivier lived here when his father was Rector of Letchworth Parish between 1918 and 1924.

★ Michael Winner, film director, attended St Christopher School before going on to Cambridge University.

★ Lenny Henry and Dawn French were once residents of Letchworth.

★ Simon West, director of films such as *Con Air* and *Lara Croft: Tomb Raider*, was born in Letchworth.

WELWYN GARDEN CITY

TOASTER: ANDY THE FIREMAN

FAVOURITE FACTS

- The Cherry Tree pub in Welwyn famously had Led Zep,
  Fleetwood Mac, Dave Dee, etc. play there in the late sixties.

- We're the second Garden City – Letchworth was the
  f***ed-up first attempt.

- The sports TV series *Superstars* was filmed at our Gosling
  Stadium from 1976 to 1983.

- Shredded Wheat is made at our Nabisco factory, which
  is also a grade 2 listed building.

- It's historically been home to many multinational HQs –
  belonging to such massive companies as ICI, SmithKline
  & French (SKF), Smith & Nephew (S&N), Roche Products,
  Polycell and Polypenco.

****

- The local Homestead Court Hotel used be where the England football team stayed for home games in the seventies, and they used to train on my local park, the King George V playing fields.

LOCAL HEROES

★ Barry Norman

★ Nick Faldo

★ Kim Wilde

★ George Bernard Shaw

★ Louis de Soissons (architect who designed WGC).

★ Sir Ebenezer Howard (founder of the Garden City movement).

COGGESHALL

TOASTER: SUSI JACOBS

Playlist

▷ **Arthur Lee and Love** – Alone Again

FAVOURITE FACTS

➤ North-east Essex is a triangle of three villages that includes Feering, Kelvedon and Coggeshall. Coggeshall village was famous for being a centre of witch trials in 1699.

- The saying 'a Coggeshall job' was used from the seventeenth to the nineteenth centuries to mean a poor or pointless piece of work, after the reputed stupidity of its villagers. Inhabitants were famous for their ridiculous and hare-brained endeavours, such as chaining up a wheelbarrow in a shed after it had been bitten by a rabid dog, for fear it would go mad.

- In 2009 Coggeshall was runner-up in a Best Kept Graveyard competition.

- Coggeshall was a big antiques centre until recently; much of the TV series *Lovejoy* was filmed there in the eighties and early nineties.

LOCAL HEROES

★ The Prodigy hail from nearby Braintree. My husband's dog had a bit of a go at Keith Flint's dog when they were about twelve years old, and Keith apparently burst into floods of tears.

SLOUGH

Playlist

▷ **Boomtown Rats** – Rat Trap

FAVOURITE FACTS

← Tommy Cooper's brother Will used to own and run a magic shop at the end of the high street until it was burned down in the early eighties.

← According to the campaign to Protect Rural England, Slough is 'England's Least Tranquil Area'.

← Slough is reckoned to be home to the biggest rats in the UK thanks to the now unused Victorian sewerage system.

← Slough is an anagram of 'Ghouls'.

LOCAL HEROES

★ Jimmy Carr

★ Ulrika Jonsson

★ Ali G now says he's from Staines, but check out his first ever TV appearance, because he boasted he was from the Slough Massive.

NAZEING

What can we say about Nazeing? It looks bloody lovely on pictures, that's for sure, and it was once, according to Rich Thrift, 'the largest village in England'. It was definitely the ONLY village in England to have won England's Greatest Village Award two years running, in 1971 and 1972. As I was born in 1972, I have decided to change my name by deedpoll to SHAUN WILLIAM KEAVENY, TWINNED WITH NAZEING, WINNER OF ENGLAND'S GREATEST VILLAGE 1971 AND 1972. Admittedly it's hard to fit on forms, etc., and my wife Lucy doesn't think much of the change, but I am happy with it.

Another fact I like is that Nazeing is home to the lowest bridge in England. Surely by definition it is also, then, home to the greatest number of disgruntled high sided-vehicle and bus drivers in England? As if all this wasn't impressive enough, Nazeing was *also* the place Cliff Richard's mum called home, back in the day. Despite the fact that Cliff has sold in excess of 175 million albums over his 130 years in show business, I feel sure that he endures much the same conversations with his mother, as many of us do . . .

CLIFF: Erm, hi, uh, ma. I'm going out on the town!
CLIFF'S MUM: In those loud trousers? And those ROLLERSKATES? Oh Cliff, you're nearly seventy. You'll go right under a bus! Can't you just use the car?

(© Shaun Keaveny 2010. This is an excerpt from my upcoming novel, *Cliff's Edge*, a fictionalization of the relationship between Cliff and the women in his life.)

****

SHAUN SEZ: If Nazeing ever needs a new slogan to boost civic pride, may I suggest 'Amazing Nazeing!'?

Playlist

▷ **Red Hot Chilli Peppers** – Under The Bridge

FAVOURITE FACTS

- Nazeing was once the largest village in England.

- Apparently it's also home to the lowest bridge in England. The bridge runs under a railway track that was once used in a scene in a TV cop show (I think it was *Juliet Bravo*).

LOCAL HEROES

★ Cliff Richard's mum lived in the area, and Cliff spent some time here.

★ Chas and Dave used to live in Nazeing.

SHAUN SEZ: Their monster 1982 hit 'Ain't No Pleasin' You' was, and if I am embarrassingly honest, still is, one of my favourite songs of all time. When I eventually interviewed the great Chas he explained the song was written from the perspective of his brother-in-law, whose marriage was nearing meltdown at the time. One day after he'd put up some curtain rails on the instruction of his wife, she came home, only to criticize his handiwork. His reaction was 'There ain't no f***in' pleasin' you!')

SWINDON

TOASTER: DANIEL MURRAY

Playlist

▷ **XTC** – Making Plans For Nigel

FAVOURITE FACTS

- The Magic Roundabout in Swindon is the seventh most feared road junction in Britain.

- Noel Gallagher roadied for the Inspiral Carpets (who had named themselves after a shop on their local estate) when they played a leisure centre here. While in Swindon he decided to name his band after said leisure centre – The Oasis.

- Swindon is referenced in Spinal Tap's 'Diva Fever'.

LOCAL HEROES

★ XTC are from, and were formed in, Swindon.

★ Julian Clary

★ Mark Lamarr

★ Gilbert O'Sullivan

★ Billie Piper

MALMESBURY

Tabloid sensationalism now dogs our collective psyche. It explains why many older people are nervous about leaving the house, why we're increasingly interested in what size nipples certain celebrities have, and why Rupert Murdoch is so rich it takes four servants a whole hour to pull on his solid gold underpants.

Despite the exponential increase in tittle-tattle, toss, titillation and terror flashing across our retinas, and the stories about KNIFE DEATHS!! GUN-WIELDING TEEN GANGS!! and BROKEN BRITAIN!! we read on an hourly basis, there is no getting away from the plain fact that many parts of Britain are, in total contrast, safe, comfortable, pedestrian, even boring. This is brilliantly illustrated in this Toast courtesy of Paul who lives in the 'sleepy' village of Malmesbury. Just imagine living in a village *so* unused to violent crime that its newspaper describes two teenagers tipping over a flower basket as a 'RIOT!' Frankly I too want to live in a village where an expired car tax disc makes page three of the local gazette. It certainly makes a change of pace from 'Feral Youths Stalk a Neighbourhood in Fear'!

In celebration of our nation's quieter backwaters, here are some absolutely true local newspaper headlines:

BED DELIVERED – UP LADDER – *Whitby Gazette*
BADGER SHOT BY ST IVES LOCKSMITH – *Cornishman*
CHAIR DESTROYED – *Westmorland Gazette*

and my personal favourite:

OVEN REMOVED FROM HOME – *Isle of Wight County Press*

****

TOASTER: PAUL RADFORD

FAVOURITE FACTS

- 'RIOT!' – This was the headline in the local newspaper the day after a couple of teenagers tipped over a flower basket.

- Dyson used to make their vacuum cleaners here.

- Malmesbury is historically 'famous' for being where a mad monk called Elmer tried to fly from the top of Malmesbury Abbey. He broke both of his legs but survived and lived to a great age.

- We're also *infamous* for the escaping pigs incident, where two pigs escaped from a slaughterhouse. It was eventually made into a TV film (might even have been BBC, I think it was called *The Tamworth Two*).

- The Second World War series *Piece of Cake* was filmed there in the eighties because the town 'looked French'.

- Despite all of the above amazing facts, it is a very sleepy place. Nothing ever happens here.

LOCAL HEROES

★ Elmer the Monk

★ William of Malmesbury, author of several texts, including *Deeds of the English Kings*, one of the earliest chronicles of English history.

****

ORPINGTON

TOASTER: JAMES WILKINS

Playlist

▷ **Mystery Jets (ft Laura Marling)** – Young Love (an ode to Orpington's own airfield, 'Biggin Hill')

FAVOURITE FACTS

- Orpington is famed for having its own eponymous breed of hen. There are several varieties, including the 'buff', 'black' and 'speckled' Orpington hen. They were first bred in the 1890s and are such pretty birds that they're often used as show birds rather than eaten!

****

- An Orpington curry house was once featured on TV as being 'one of the worst in the country'.

- Biggin Hill airfield was one of the commanding bases for the Battle of Britain in the Second World War. One of the runways also appears on the back cover of Pink Floyd's 1969 album *Ummagumma*.

- Orpington featured in a Honda ad in 2006 which showed a bunch of Mexican villagers watching footage on a projector of someone driving round the town. It finished with the words, 'Of course you're adventurous. You just live in Orpington.' We're not sure whether we should be insulted by this.

LOCAL HEROES

★ Past residents include Charles Darwin and Jeremy Beadle, who went to school with my dad.

THE BOURNE, FARNHAM

It was in his car that he felt safest of all, as plastercast-pasty pop prince Gary Numan bleated back in 1979 on his superhit 'Cars'. He told me once during an interview that he indeed *did* feel safe in his car at that time, as a combination of Asperger's Syndrome and vertiginous and immediate fame had left him somewhat agoraphobic. Of course, cars can be hazardous places, and Colin's car-centric Toast reminds us of this. The Bourne played host to the construction of the first British car, but also, perhaps inevitably, the first accident, *and* Britain's first speeding ticket. The curious mind cannot help but imagine what it must have been like to have been issued with the first ever speeding ticket...

(*Interlude of harp music denoting falling into a vivid reverie*)
POLICEMAN (*peddling furiously*): Please (puff!) pull over, sir! Command this horseless carriage to cease in the first instance!
BRITAIN'S FIRST TRAFFIC FELON (*possibly sounding/looking like Terry-Thomas*): Hello, old chap, can I help you at all?
POLICEMAN (*regaining composure*): Step away from the self-propelling transport box please, sir.
BFTF: Certainly, old bean.
POLICEMAN: *Well, hello mister racehorse!* Do you have *any idea* how fast you were going back there in that five zone?

****

BFTF: I'm sure I don't.

POLICEMAN: FIFTEEN MILES PER HOUR, SIR! THAT'S FASTER THAN A COW ON A SKATEBOARD GOING DOWNHILL! Can I take your registration number please?

BFTF: One.

POLICEMAN: Now, if I catch you going that fast again I will have no choice but to put three points on your licence. I will let you off this time, as I have come out without my quill and inkwell. Think yourself lucky!

TOASTER: COLIN HAMMOND

Playlist

▷ **Mungo Jerry** – In The Summer Time

FAVOURITE FACTS

- The opening battle scene from *Gladiator* (and lots of other stuff besides) was filmed in Bourne Woods.

- The car crash in Coldplay's video for 'The Scientist' was filmed in Bourne Woods as well. This is sort of fitting, because the first British car was built in Farnham, which was followed shortly by the first road traffic accident and the first traffic ticket, which also occurred in the locality.

LOCAL HEROES

★ J. M. Barrie (author of *Peter Pan*) lived in the Bourne Woods.

****

★ Jonny Wilkinson, Graham Thorpe and Mike Hawthorn also hail from nearby.

SHAUN SEZ: A source of endless mirth to my wife and me is that our little bundle of comedy, Arthur (two years old at time of going to press) tends to adopt a position identical to Wilkinson's 'ball kicking' one when he is pushing out a poo. Arms out front – hands clasped – look of intense concentration. Difference is, Arthur's conversion rate is 100 per cent. I am sure he will thank me for including this scatological reminiscence when he reads this at eighteen.

★ Apparently Mungo Jerry lived in Farnham too.

ELY

TOASTER: CHRISTINE JONES

> **Playlist**
>
> ▷ **Eels** – Beautiful Freak (which sums Ely up nicely)

FAVOURITE FACTS

➤ Ely is the third-smallest city in England – only Wells and the City of London are smaller.

➤ Previously known as the Isle of Ely, the city was an island up until the seventeenth century, when the Fens were drained.

➤ Highlights in the calendar include the Elysian beer festival in late February and Ely Eel Day in May, which celebrates the city's namesake, the eel. There's a parade, then an eel-throwing competition.

****

- Ely was once home to Britain's fattest Labrador, but after the publicity it received when this was found out, it slimmed down to a normal-sized dog.

- Ely is the only other place other than on the Thames where the Oxford–Cambridge boat race has been held, which was during the Second World War.

LOCAL HEROES

★ Sir Clive Woodward, Rugby World Cup-winning manager.

★ Guy Pearce, from *LA Confidential* and *The Proposition*, lived here for a while.

★ Andrew Eldritch from The Sisters Of Mercy.

HASTINGS

OK, here's a quick quiz. You buy a carton of orange juice. What is contained in the carton? Is it A: orange juice, B: tomato juice or C: a unicorn's tears? You would be forgiven for answering A. But as we can see from Jo White's Toast, things are often far from what they seem.

Who among us knew that the iconic battle of battles, skirmishes of skirmishes, scrap to end all military scraps, the Battle of Hastings, was *in fact* conducted in Battle, six miles down the road? NO! Me neither! What on *earth* were the historians thinking? Did they start documenting the bloody events of the *Battle of Battle*, and then think, 'Hang on, that sounds a bit stupid!' before plumping for a place name down the road? Might the epic battle have even ended up being known as the *Battle of St Leonards on Sea*?

This poses a wider question: how many of our other great battles of the ages were *really* fought where the title suggests? *Was* the Battle of 'Britain' *really* fought here?

Jo also reveals that John Logie Baird invented television whilst while on hols in Hastings. (Quite industrious of him. Usually all I manage is a few lengths of the hotel pool and a Maeve Binchy.) Sadly we do not have time or space here to debate whether, in harsh retrospect, television has been a boon or a burden to the world over the last century, but one thing is for shiz: without that holiday in Hastings, there'd be no *Snog Marry Avoid*, Ben Shephard or seasons one to sixteen of *Two Pints of Lager and a Packet of Crisps*.

Playlist

▷ **Blur** – Coffee And TV

▷ **Acoustic Ladyland** – Cuts and Lies
(they're a homegrown band)

FAVOURITE FACTS

- The obvious one is the Battle of Hastings, which actually wasn't in Hastings but in the town of Battle a few miles up the road. William just hung out here prior to the battle, stuck Harold one in the eye and then built a castle in Hastings.

- John Logie Baird came to Hastings to convalesce in 1923. While he was here he did experiments and eventually created grainy pictures of a Maltese Cross (the same shape as the St John Ambulance medal, in case you know what that looks like), which became the first broadcast images. There are signs coming into Hastings claiming it is the 'birthplace of television'.

****

- There has been a fishing fleet in Hastings for over 600 years and it is the largest beach-launched fleet in the country.

- The East Hill lift in Hastings is the steepest funicular railway in the country. At least we think it is.

LOCAL HEROES

★ Jo Brand

★ Catherine Cookson

★ Harry H. Corbett

★ Aleister Crowley, famed author and occultist.

★ Desmond Llewellyn – Q from the Bond films.

PLYMPTON

Corin's Toast below is a relatively workmanlike affair, basing itself mainly around the historical fact (unsubstantiated by me) that some of those Pilgrim Fathers might have set sail from the dock in the town. This is now the third place that's claimed that this happened there! Who'll be next?

There's also a nice Laurel and Hardy titbit, but the one we're all really drawn to is the food-based fact. Corin blithely points out that Plympton is the birthplace of some of the nation's most treasured snacks, such as the Bourbon Cream, the Garibaldi biscuit and, most impressively, the mighty Twiglet (oxymoron alert?). Now THAT is a claim to fame if ever I saw one! Which one of us that calls ourselves British has NOT at some point shared a plate of Bourbons in an unspoken act of inter-generational bonding with a grandparent? Which one of us *so-called Brits* has NOT piled up a corner of a paper plate at a buffet with Twiglets, making it look like some kind of Action Man-sized firewood pyre?

Corin concludes his Toast with a sad signoff, 'no Local Heroes'. This could be the beginnings of a great Stranglers lyric, but it is instead is a sad indictment of the harrowing lack of respect given in general to those brave, innovative and tirelessly toiling geniuses that are, every day, inventing many and varied new ways for us, the nation, to enjoy fats, carbohydrates and salt. I am talking about those most unsung of men, THE SNACK INVENTORS! (Fade up the *Escape to Victory* soundtrack.) How can we live in a society in which the man, the LEGEND, who first combined wheat-based protein and yeast extract to

****

make a delicious if thirst-inducing twiglike treat is NOT recognized with a statue or at the very least a street name? Why is the person who pioneered the alchemical confluence of nougat, caramel and chocolate to make the Mars bar NOT celebrated with a 70-metre statue similar to the one Christ has in Rio? WHY?

I sometimes think I feel *too much.*

TOASTER: CORIN DENTON

Playlist

▷ **The Shins** – Sea Legs

FAVOURITE FACTS

☛ In the sixteenth century Pilgrims left for America and from here, and now Americans frequently come over to visit the Mayflower steps. However there's another more recent pier that they always stand on – so nearly all of them come 6,000 miles only to take pictures standing on the wrong steps. The actual steps are under the ladies toilets at the pub over the road.

☛ The British Fireworks Championships are held here.

SHAUN SEZ: They should kill two birds with one stone and also host The National Most Nervous Pet Championships here too.

****

- The Palace Theatre in Plympton is the last place Laurel and Hardy performed together.

- For some reason we have a rich history of snack invention – Twiglets, the Bourbon and Garibaldi biscuits were all invented here.

TROWBRIDGE

TOASTER: SARAH COLLINS

Playlist

▷ **Tears for Fears** – Changes (Trowbridge is slowly changing; we were supposed to get a Waitrose until they pulled out, and we may soon get a cinema – ooh!)

FAVOURITE FACTS

- In 1820, Trowbridge was dubbed the 'Manchester of the West' due to the number of factories and mills here.

- Bowyers made pork pies here, but the factory had to close in 2008 as, due to EU rulings, Melton Mowbray pork pies have to be made in Melton Mowbray.

- Performers to appear at the legendary 'Psychic Pig' club include Supergrass and P. J. Harvey. The club paid £50 for a band called Only On A Friday, who insisted on being billed as 'Radiohead' on the night as they had changed their name.

- There was a recording studio nearby owned originally by Tears For Fears, where the Smiths recorded in the eighties. I had to serve tea to Morrissey and the boys whilst working at a local tea shop. I was a massive fan and had to get Mozzer to sign the visitors' book.

LOCAL HEROES

★ Sir Isaac Pitman, inventor of shorthand, was born here.

****

AYLESBURY

Aylesbury. A delightful and very English town north of Oxford. Unremarkable perhaps, apart from its eponymous ducks. But as always, our Toasters never fail to lift the lid on some red-hot and previously unknown factage. Here Keith seems rightly proud of one of Ayelsbury's standout facts, that Aylesbury was *the first place in the world to get its own railway branch line in 1839*. Impressive? Indeed yes. But you can BET those Aylesburians have been dining out on that one for over a century and a half. Imagine the poor people of towns adjacent to mighty Aylesbury being assailed constantly by reminders of that stellar rail-related fact. 'Excellent swordfish, Maisie . . . by the way, did you know that our little town of Aylesbury was the first IN THE WORLD to get its own railway branch line?'

'Yes, yes, bloody yes! You mentioned it the second you arrived and then during the first course!'

Of course, we are prevaricating around the bush here. As the ultimate Aylesbury fact is clear to all. That leather-lunged, male-pattern-baldness-suffering, pop prog master and Peter Gabriel soundalike Fish (Derek Dick) is a resident and once worked in the unemployment office. WOW! For the record, I have to admit to you that our Orms and myself were colossal Marillion fans back in the day. We pored with religious fervour over every hackneyed sixth-form couplet, every chiming chorus-drenched Rothery guitar part, every Harlequin-adorned album sleeve. We would even listen to the whole seventeen medieval minutes of

'Grendel'! We were superfans. Somewhere in the world, extant, there lies a dusty C60 Maxell tape that contains a performance of Marillion's 'Punch And Judy', sung lustily and tunelessly (much like the great man himself) by myself and Orms into a condenser mike slung over a light fitting. We would often muse over the significance of Derek's name change to Fish. Apparently to this day Fish's mum, Mrs Dick, will not accept the name change.

TOASTER: KEITH REDWORTH

Playlist

▷ **Marillion** – Market Square Heroes (very much a local band. Fish used to work in the local unemployment benefit office)

FAVOURITE FACTS

- Aylesbury is the county town of Bucks. Its name comes from the Anglo Saxon *aigle burgh*, which means 'hill town'.

- It was the first place in the world to get its own railway branch line in 1839.

- It is the birthplace of the paralympics, which were pioneered by Sir Ludwig Guttmann. The first ever games for wheelchair athletics were held here in 1954.

- The local court heard the trials of the great train robbers in the sixties (both their hideout and the place of the robbery were nearby). The BBC now use the court for *Judge John Deed*.

****

- It's famous for its ducks, which are white with an orange beak and still live on the local canal – people born in the town are known as Aylesbury ducks (and are rumoured to all have webbed feet).

LOCAL HEROES

★ David Jason

★ John Junkin, actor, writer and voice of one of the chimps in the PG Tips ads.

★ Wild Willy Barrett and John Otway (headbutts).

(to name but a few)

ROYAL
TUNBRIDGE WELLS

The royals, in general, love posh stuff. That is their taste. It isn't that they're being snobby or owt, it's just the way they have been brought up. Poshness is their *reality*. My dad always used to say the Queen thought everything just naturally smelled of fresh paint, due to the millions of minions feverishly retouching every surface just before her arrival. It's a basic rule of thumb that if you ask, say, Princess Michael of Kent whether she'd like foie gras with date purée and pomegranate or a scotch egg, she is likely to go for the former. (That said there are exceptions to these rules of thumb. Apparently Princess Diana liked nothing better than a greasy kebab, and Albert, Prince of Monaco, has a three-a-day Bombay Bad Boy Pot Noodle habit.)

And so it is that we alight upon the Toast for ROYAL Tunbridge Wells. As you will see below, ROYAL Tunbridge Wells was bestowed with this grand honour when the patron saint of potatoes, King Edward VII, 'officially recognized its popularity with the royals' back in the early 1900s. Whether this was done officially, by way of a letter and royal charter, or unofficially, simply by him shouting, 'I fuggin love thiss place, I doo!' after a few lager tops in a local hostelry, we will never know. Either way, Tunbridge, like the equally grandiosely named Royal Leamington Spa before it, can now look haughtily and disparagingly down on every other so-called conurbation in Britain from its royal-appointed ivory tower.

****

To be honest, many places in Britain, though perhaps worthy of a royal seal of approval, wouldn't *sound* right with the 'royal' prefix. Here are some examples of that:

1 Royal Wigan
2 Royal Scunthorpe
3 Royal Barnsley
4 Royal Dagenham
5 Royal Tooting

TOASTERS: SUE & PAUL WEBSTER

Playlist

▷ **The Pogues** – Dirty Old Town

▷ **The Who** – Won't Get Fooled Again

▷ **Sex Pistols** – Anarchy In The UK

FAVOURITE FACTS

- Tunbridge Wells became 'Royal' in 1909 when King Edward VII officially recognized its popularity with the royals and aristocracy alike. It is one of only two towns to be granted this, the other being Leamington Spa. Tunbridge Wells became a spa town in Georgian times and had its heyday as a tourist resort under Richard 'Beau' Nash, a celebrated dandy and leader of fashion.

- Tunbridge Wells has a reputation as being archetypal 'Middle England', a stereotype typified by the fictional letter writer who signs himself 'Disgusted of Tunbridge Wells'. This is thought to date back to the fifties, when the newspaper editor of the *Tunbridge Wells Advertiser* became alarmed at the lack of letters from readers and insisted his staff write a few to fill spaces. One of them signed off 'Disgusted of Tunbridge Wells'.

- Roger Daltrey has a trout farm on the town's outskirts.

SHAUN SEZ: I have interviewed the Great Rog thrice now, and each time forgotten to deliver the killer question: 'How are your trouts?' He did once tell me, though, after I had him sign my ukulele, that despite writing 'Blue Red And Grey' on a uke, Pete Townshend refused to use one onstage as he reckoned it would make him look a right twerp.

- After three hours of spectacular sprawling desert and heat-shimmering wilderness, David Lean's epic *Lawrence of Arabia* makes mention of Tunbridge Wells in its last line. It closes with Mr Dryden answering King Feisal: 'Me, your highness? On the whole, I wish I'd stayed in Tunbridge Wells.'

- Local music venue The Forum is a former Art Deco lavatory. It used to be the largest public convenience in Europe. In recent years it has hosted gigs by the likes of The Libertines, Glasvegas, Biffy Clyro, Feeder, Bloc Party and We Are Scientists.

LOCAL HEROES

★ Sid Vicious

★ Shane MacGowan

★ Tom Baker

★ Jilly Goolden

★ Jo Brand

CRANLEIGH

TOASTER: ADAM ABRAHAMS

FAVOURITE FACTS

- The name Cranleigh originates from Crane Ley, which means a place where long, heronesque birds live. It's the biggest village in the UK and sits halfway between London and Brighton close to the Surrey/West Sussex border.

- It also has Britain's oldest village hospital, though it's used to house the elderly as opposed to offering medical treatment.

- Oliver Cromwell used it as a stop-off point and stationed a garrison there. In memory of this we have the inappropriately quaint Cromwell Tea Room.

- Bonfire Night is a huge local event – it attracts about 20,000 visitors with a torch procession and impressive firework display. *The Star Wars* theme is also played in time with the explosions.

LOCAL HEROES

★ Ringo Starr lives here. His estate has one of the oldest walled gardens in Britain. I once had a conversation with him about how koala bears get stoned.

★ Eric Clapton, Jodie Kidd, Alvin Stardust and Kenny Jones are all regular Cranleigh shoppers.

★ When Anthea Turner lit the Cranleigh bonfire one year there were calls from the crowd to 'Burn her'. The chant was allegedly being led by her husband.

HAYLE

Pasties. OK you got me. Pasties, in fact let's broaden this, *pastry* in general, are one of my favourite past(ie)imes. As Zellweger's wan and loathsome character in the film *Jerry Maguire* cheesily choked, 'You had me at "hello",' I might be heard to say, in equally emotive tones, 'You had me at "pastie".' The Toaster in charge of representing Hayle in Cornwall strikes this rich seam by telling us about Hayle's Philips Pasties, by all accounts *the ultimate* pasty purveyors of this fair isle. As we all know there are many hands a-clamourin' for that little accolade, but upon inspection it seems that it may not just have been hubris on the part of Jo, as, if you pop 'Philips Pasties' into YouTube, you will find there, an eight-minute video of a very serious man in a wetsuit (?) purchasing, consuming and favourably critiquing his pastry purchase.

To many, the idea of filming oneself eating and reviewing a pasty might seem barmy. To me, it seems not only a good idea, but the basis of a sweeping, big-budget twenty-part BBC documentary entitled *Around the World in Eighty Pies with Shaun Keaveny* (no interest from production companies at time of going to press).

Notice that, as well as the pasty thing, Jo mentions the fact (in the Famous Faces section) that Kate Winslet has sometimes been spotted 'at car boots' in the area. Notice that, when we are Toasting the Nation, we require less substantiation and verification than, say, the Passport Office. A Toaster's word is good enough for us. If someone says, 'I think I saw actress Kate Hudson going through my recycling bins last night,' who are we to contradict?

****

TOASTER: JOE BEER

> **Playlist**
>
> ▷ **Rosie And The Goldbug** – Soldier Blue
> (most popular local band)

FAVOURITE FACTS

- In the Bronze Age Hayle was used as a port for the shipping of tin, which was used for tools and weapons at the time and continued until the Iron Age.

- In my spare time I am a Keanu Reeves lookalike. Whether this says anything about the place or not I don't know.

> **SHAUN SEZ:** That's quite a claim, isn't it? We were given no photographic evidence to corroborate Joe's likeness, but it at least suggests he is a fairly good-looking man. My brother reckons I could scrape a living as a Trent Reznor lookalike should the work dry up. It's always nice to have something to fall back on in this fickle business.

- In the 1850s Hayle was again the industrial capital of Cornwall – the coal piles on the dockside were bigger than houses next to them.

LOCAL HEROES

★ Rick Reolla – lost his life on 9/11 after rescuing others then returning to the towers.

★ Nigel Terry – played King Arthur in *Excalibur*, also starred as a priest in *Troy*.

★ Kate Winslet – has been seen at local car boot sales.

SOUTHEND-ON-SEA

TOASTER: DOM MAGUIRE

FAVOURITE FACTS

- We have the longest pleasure pier in the world. Ships have collided with it twice and it has burned down three times in my lifetime, hence the summer/autumn expression in these parts: 'The air hangs heavy with the smell of burning pier.'

- For years, Southend Tourist Board's strapline was 'Southend-on-Sea – the Place to Be'. We are not actually '-on-Sea', though – we are on the muddy banks of the Thames Estuary. The beaches are man-made.

- Southend United are the only league team in Britain to have a 100 per cent win record against Manchester United (7 November 2006: Southend 1 Man Utd 0).

- *EastEnders* characters routinely escape to Southend when things get tough in Albert Square.

- The video for Mozza's 'Every Day Is Like Sunday' was shot on Southend's beaches and in Golden Disc records. My sister tried to get in on the shoot and failed.

- We're twinned with the Polish port of Sopot. Thrillingly, it has the longest wooden pier in Europe.

LOCAL HEROES

★ Radio 2 DJ Steve Wright went to local Eastwood School.

★ Musicians connected with Southend: Procul Harum; Talk Talk; Dr Feelgood (well, Canvey Island); that gurning one out of Busted; Phill Burdett; and, lest we forget, the hugely talented Menswear.

CANTERBURY

'SIMPLY INSPIRATIONAL'
canterbury.co.uk

TOASTER: TOM WHITE

Playlist

▷ **Luke Smith** – She's A Do-Er

▷ **Ian Dury** – Sex & Drugs & Rock & Roll

FAVOURITE FACTS

- Canterbury is known as the Mother of England due to Canterbury Cathedral being the mother church of the Anglican Community.

- The word 'canter' comes from Canterbury, originating from the Canterbury Trot, which is faster than a trot but less tiring than a gallop.

- King's School, Canterbury, established in AD 600, is almost certainly one of the oldest in the country.

- Smallfilms Productions was established by Oliver Postgate and Peter Firmin in a cowshed on the outskirts of Canterbury in 1959 and created the likes of *Bagpuss*, *The Clangers*, *Noggin the Nog* and *Ivor the Engine*.

LOCAL HEROES

★ Former pupils of King's School include David Gough, Orlando Bloom and Christopher Marlowe (the local theatre, the most hideous building in the city, is named after him).

★ Jodie Kidd was born here.

★ Ian Dury took a position teaching and lecturing in art at Canterbury Art College in 1967 – around the time he started writing and performing his music.

★ Ian Fleming died of a heart attack in Canterbury Hospital in 1964.

MAIDSTONE

FAVOURITE FACTS

- Maidstone is the county town of Kent in the heart of the Garden of England.

- The World Custard Pie Throwing Championships are also held in the local Mote Park, and last year it was the fortieth anniversary. It includes events such as Wellie Throwing, the National Skipping Championships and Egg Throwing. All the teams wear fancy dress.

- Sharps toffee factory, which made Liquorice Allsorts, used to be based in the town. And we used to have a huge hop-growing tradition, serving the brewing trade.

- We've also got Leeds Castle, 900 years old and built on two islands on the River Len. Henry VIII used to visit regularly and did it up for his first wife, Catherine of Aragon. It has hosted loads of outdoor concerts, including Elton John and James Blunt. The *Dr Who* episode 'Androids of Tara' was filmed there too.

LOCAL HEROES

★ Agony aunt and TV personality Anne Widdecombe is the local MP.

★ Benjamin Disraeli, who was distantly related to George Washington, was first the local MP and later Prime Minister.

★ Lord Beaverbrook went to Maidstone Grammar School and William Golding, author of *Lord of the Flies*, used to teach there.

★ Tracy Emin started her art career at the art college.

★ Both Ross Kemp and Barry from *EastEnders* and Tom Baker, the fourth Dr Who, also came from Maidstone.

BILLERICAY

**'I JUST KNOW YOU WILL BE SURPRISED HOW
RICH THE HISTORY OF BILLERICAY IS'**

billericay.net

TOASTER: JUDITH

Playlist

▷ **Ian Dury and The Blockheads** – Billericay Dickie

FAVOURITE FACTS

- In 1916 a German Zeppelin airship was famously gunned down over Billericay, and narrowly missed the high street when it fell.

- King Harold's dad lived in Great Burstead, which Billericay used to be a part of.

****

R2D2 LIVES IN PRESTON

- It's a very old town, with links to the Bronze and Iron Ages, and was occupied by the Romans and Saxons.

- We have historical links to the *Mayflower* voyage as five of its residents were on the ship; however, only one survived the winter when they got there!

LOCAL HEROES

★ Lee Evans

★ Alison Moyet

★ Darren Day

★ Francis Thomas Bacon

★ Shane Ritchie

★ Stephen George Ritchie (from Die Toten Hosen) and one member of Depeche Mode.

CHIPPING NORTON

'FONDLY KNOWN AS "CHIPPY" BY THE LOCALS'
cotswolds.info

TOASTER: PETER EDDERSHAW

Playlist

▷ **Dexys Midnight Runners** – Dance Stance

FAVOURITE FACTS

▬ Chipping Norton Recording Studios have played host to various rock glitterati, including the Bay City Rollers and Gerry Rafferty. Dexys Midnight Runners recorded their debut album at the studios but 'kidnapped' the master tapes from the car park outside the studios.

▬ Keith Moon used to own the Crown and Cushion Hotel on the high street.

▬ Ronnie Barker had an antiques shop here! Apparently the *Sun* tried to claim that Ronnie had deliberately undervalued some priceless antique that the *Sun* were pretending to sell. Ronnie went on the *Wogan* show to complain about the *Sun*'s behaviour.

BRISTOL

TOASTERS: ANNA TIMMS
NEILL TRABBLE

FAVOURITE FACTS

➤ Ribena, tarmac and the Plimsoll line were all invented in Bristol.

➤ Bristol also has two famous dogs: Nipper, the dog on the HMV logo, was born in Bristol, and Wallace's mate Gromit is another local lad.

➤ Two famous characters are from here: Lara Croft was created by Bristol-based artist Toby Gard; and apparently Harry Potter was based on a young boy that J. K. Rowling met in Bristol when she was a young girl.

****

- Toaster Neill: in *The Young Ones* there is a scene in the final episode where they rob a bank, and you can see the bank from my window!

- *Only Fools and Horses* – Nelson Mandela House exteriors were filmed in Bedminster, or Bemmie as it is affectionately known, and the famous Batman and Robin scene was filmed in Bristol too.

LOCAL HEROES

★ Famous Bristolians range from Johnny Ball and Vicki Pollard to Banksy and the lovely Stephen Merchant.

★ Famous Bristol bands/musicians include Bananarama, Russ Conway, Massive Attack, Roni Size, Portishead and Goldie.

HATFIELD

In Jonny's Toast of Hatfield he mentions The Police and Sting. Poor old Sting. Despite his many millions, his enviably stable second marriage and his secure position towards the top of the great songwriters' pecking order, he *still* manages to be a bit of a joke. I guess in many ways we're all just a bit jealous of him, and so decide to prick his perceived pomposity with a few well-aimed kicks in the balls. With that in mind, here are some annoying things about Sting:

1 *Sting's claims vis-à-vis Tantric sexual prowess.* In the eighties he claimed that he and his wife Trudie had Tantric sex for up to eight hours at a time. This is apparently true. To alleviate the boredom, Trudie had a 40-inch TV mounted on the ceiling of their bedroom so she could watch *Dallas* while the Stingster omm'ed to climax.

2 *Sting has recorded some sixteenth-century lute music.* In 2008 Sting released, not an album, but 'an arc of songs that conjure the season of spirits, the eerie silences of the snow; days of solitude and reflection for some, a time of re-birth and celebration for many'. Or, as Noddy Holder more succinctly put it, 'EEEEET'S CHRIIIIIIISSSSSTMAAAAAASSS!' Big props to Sting for learning the lute, which is a rare medieval instrument. He found his for a good price in *Lute* magazine. (Cue tumbleweed.)

****

3 *Sting goes on about deforestation and carbon emissions whilst doing Jaguar car ads and flying about in a private jet.* Then again, as my nan would say, 'At least he's having a try.'

Here is a little-known fact no one seems to know about Sting. The Police's superhit 'Every Little Thing She Does Is Magic' was actually commissioned by Paul Daniels for his new wife Debbie McGee. There is a version recorded by Paul on his little-remembered 1984 double album of 'seductive future classics' entitled *Debbie Does Daniels*. If you're lucky enough to locate a copy (last I heard copies were going for £200 a time on eBay) you could enjoy tracks like '(I'm In) The Magic Circle', 'Rub My Magic Wand' and Paul's incendiary jazz-funk version of 'Let's Get It On'.

TOASTER: JONNY MILLS

Playlist

▷ **Free** – Alright Now

FAVOURITE FACTS

- The Police played *Rock Goes to College* at Hatfield Polytechnic 21 February 1979, which included the first live performance of 'Message In A Bottle'.

- Former guitarist with The Rolling Stones Mick Taylor grew up in Hatfield.

- *Saving Private Ryan* and *Band of Brothers* were filmed on location at the Hatfield Aerospace Factory.

- Apparently Adam Ant's 'Stand And Deliver' video was filmed in Hatfield too.

LOCAL HEROES

★ The lead singer of The Zombies, Colin Blunstone, grew up here, and apparently Tracey Thorn did too.

SHAUN SEZ: I once saw Tracey Thorn and her brother at a party back in the day. Seated awkwardly between them with little to say for himself was mop-topped and enigmatic Gretsch-botherer John Squire. I guess you could say he was . . . a rose between two thorns! Ha! Wait — STOP . . . THROWING . . . THOSE . . . SHOES . . . AT . . . ME!

CHELTENHAM

Where on *earth* would tabloid journalists be without the Heath and Safety Executive? For 'tis they that provide the *Mail*, *Mirror*, *Sun* and *Star* with (at the last academic calculation) 38 per cent of their daily material for stories. Recently on the show we talked about the fact that one of Britain's greatest and silliest traditions, the Cheltenham cheese-rolling event (see below), had to be cancelled due once again to that pariah of modern-day fun, the Health and Safety Executive. Gutted by the cheesy stink created by the banning, a local councillor implored, 'Cheese rolling has been going on for hundreds of years and we must ensure that this great tradition continues.' (At the time of going to press, the council are looking to a compromise which will be the annual Cheltenham cheese-slice-tossing event, but by all accounts this has not satisfied the roller traditionalists.)

Of course, the cry of IT'S ELF AN SAFETY GAWN MAAAD! is one we hear with increasing regularity. We all recall the furore created when certain schools attempted to ban the game of conkers, but who remembers the nervy council that got one local daredevil to change the name of his 'Wall of Death' attraction to the 'Gradient of Considerable Peril'? One local council who cannot be named for legal reasons are trying to implement a by-law stating that it is illegal to get pregnant in their borough, as birth leads at some point to definite death. To quote from their latest press release, 'a direct and incontrovertible link has now been established between birth and death. Therefore the act of copulation with a view to birth is to be outlawed in order to put a stop to this epidemic of death in our towns.' When you think about it, they have a point.

TOASTER: DAVID

Playlist

▷ **Billy Bragg** – The Saturday Boy (Cheltenham was where I first saw Billy performing, in 1984 or 1985, during the annual march in support of the trade union members made jobless by Thatcher during her reign of terror)

FAVOURITE FACTS

- Cheltenham seems to have an incredible number of festivals: blues, jazz, folk, literature and also the National Hunt festival in March, although people still complain there is 'nothing to do'.

- Every year just outside Cheltenham there is the annual 'cheese-rolling' event, best described as insane people chasing a double Gloucester cheese off a cliff.

****

LOCAL HEROES

★ Brian Jones

> **SHAUN SEZ:** A truly underrated musician;
> it's arguable that the Stones became much
> less interesting without him. What's more,
> John Paul Jones of Led Zeppelin borrowed
> his hair in the 1976 concert movie The Song
> Remains the Same.

★ Richard O'Brien

★ 'Bomber' Harris

★ Captain Edward Wilson, who perished with Scott
  at that South Pole.

NORWICH

TOASTERS: KIRSTY
BEC CROUCH

Playlist

▷ **The Kinks** – The Village Green Preservation Society

▷ **The Communards** – Don't Leave Me This Way

FAVOURITE FACTS

➤ Kettle Chips and Coleman's mustard both originate from Norwich. It has 365 pubs (one for each day of the year) and fifty-two churches (a church for each week), apparently.

➤ The Norfolk coast is a major drug-running route into the UK!

****

- Fictional Alan Partridge spent his fictional childhood in Norwich before becoming a DJ on Radio Norwich (A-ha!). There was an equivalent to Alan Partridge on Radio Norwich, who might have inspired him – or maybe not. It's just that sort of place.

- NORWICH in the Second World War was code British soldiers used for 'Knickers Off Ready When I Come Home'.

- Our city hospital has an abbreviation for generally weird patients/symptoms – NFN, Normal for Norfolk.

LOCAL HEROES

★ Musically our most important ex-resident was William Crotch (1775–1847), known as 'Norwich's Mozart', who gave daily organ recitals.

★ Beth Orton spent much of her childhood here.

CAMBRIDGE

I don't know about you, but the first thing that springs to *my* mind when someone mentions Cambridge is the cerebral. Cloaked and mortared professors dispensing pearls to their prodigies on dew-dropped lawns while river-roving dandies in boaters quote Shelley to their winsome women.

Who knew that it is in FACT the birthplace of modern football? That it's therefore responsible for glamour model-roasting, boasting, disabled parking space-nabbing money-grabbing multi-millionaire masters of the modern game? Not me, that's for shiz.

I am a massive football fan, though. I *just cannot get enough of the game*. I LOVE it when the ball goes between the stick thingies! WAHEY! I also love it when one man has it, and then another man with a different colour on, gets it off him! YES! In your FACE! I also love listening to the dreamy Alan Handsome off of Football Focus when he talks to that one that sells crisps with the big ears. GENIUS!

One thing I heartily disapprove of in Lawrence's Toast is his Toast fact regarding the toaster that never burns toast. This is yet another example of political correctness GONE MAD! (No it isn't. Get control of yourself. Ed.) If I want to burn my toast, I AM WITHIN MY RIGHTS TO DO SO, OK? What if I like the smell of charcoal in the morning? What this manufacturer clearly hasn't considered is that I get a lot of exercise jumping up and down waving an oven glove at the smoke alarm every morning! And I LIKE IT!

****

TOASTER: LAWRENCE GRASTY

Playlist

▷ **Super Furry Animals** – Hometown Unicorn

▷ **Broken Family Band** – Love Your Man, Love Your Woman (from the *Hello Love* album)

FAVOURITE FACTS

- Cambridge is incredibly flat. There are several 'Hill' streets in the city centre – none of which have a discernible slope. This though perhaps helped Cambridge become the birthplace of modern football. Parker's Piece (park in the middle of town) is where a set of rules were set out that led to the current FA rules.

- Toast connection: local firm Cambridge Consultants have come up with a non-toast-burning toaster. It has the snappy name of Toastz ...

LOCAL HEROES

★ Broken Family Band hail from Cambridge.

★ Cambridge is the birthplace of Douglas Adams, Richard Attenborough, Christopher Cockerell (inventor of the hovercraft), David Gilmour and Syd Barrett (who returned here post-Floyd).

TOAST
WALES

CARDIFF

TOASTERS: SARAH AUSTIN
                MIKE DAVIS

Playlist

▷ **Curtis Mayfield** – We Got To Have Peace

▷ **Super Furry Animals** – Play It Cool

FAVOURITE FACTS

- Cardiff City FC are the only non-English club to have won the FA Cup (in 1927) and we nearly won again recently. All we lacked was a striker and 50 million quid.

- Cardiff is home to the UK's oldest record store, Spillers.

- *Dr Who* and *Torchwood* are both filmed in Cardiff, owing to the fact that there's a psychic rift that runs beneath the city.

- The first ever million-pound deal was struck in Cardiff (in the local Coal Exchange in 1907).

- Cardiff is the world's first Fair Trade capital city, and thirty countries have a diplomatic presence here.

- Although of Norwegian descent, world-famous author Roald Dahl was born in Cardiff! There's a public plaza named after him in the city – Roald Dahl Plass (which means plaza in Norwegian).

****

- Of the 317,500 people who live here, over 30,000 come from a minority ethnic group – we have one of the oldest-established Indian, Yemeni and Somali populations in the UK.

LOCAL HEROES

★ John Humphrys, Mr Radio 4.

★ Jeremy Bowen, one of the finest overseas/warzone/ formerly bearded correspondents the BBC has ever produced.

★ Colin Jackson, the holder of one of the longest-standing athletics world records, for the 110m hurdles. He doesn't hold the record any more, but he's still a local legend.

★ Some members of the mighty Super Furry Animals hail from here. No mention of Cardiff can be made without reference to this genius band.

ABERYSTWYTH

It is said that we are, as a civilization, in the grip of a kind of rabid mania, propagated by our exponentially increasing media outlets, to proliferate bad news stories so as to induce a nameless sense of dread within the populace, make us more open to government-sanctioned mind control, and in turn cause us to consume ever more material items to help us forget about the sewer of sub-humanity in which we dwell. Luckily, they didn't seem to get that memo in Aberystwyth, where, according to Toaster Jessica, there is little crime to write home about. Or even write in the newspaper about. Her examples of crime headlines are delightfully trivial, such as 'Pie Stolen'. Which of us *doesn't* from time to time fantasize about a news programme that for once *wasn't* chock to the clack with terror and misery, but was instead more... *Aberystwythian?*

Once again, we hear the tinkling harp music denoting a dream sequence. The News at Ten theme fades out and we see Girls Aloud's Sarah Harding, shuffling papers.
SARAH HARDING: Hiya! (*Waves. Then her face instantly turns serious.*) The news tonight . . .
BONG!
SH: A couple who thought they'd been robbed had in fact just mislaid their jewellery box and laptop.
BONG!
SH: Not *one* earthquake or landslide occurred in any foreign countries, but they had some lovely weather!
BONG!

****

SH: Robbie Williams retires from music.
BONG!
SH: That's it really . . .

TOASTER: JESSICA ADAMS

Playlist

▷ **Pet Shop Boys** – Go West (as that is how you get to Aber!)

▷ **Camera Obscura** – Let's Get Out Of This Place

▷ **The Crimea** – White Russian Galaxy

FAVOURITE FACTS

- The local population is only 12,000, but there are 7,000 students on top of that. Aberystwyth is so studious it's the home to the National Library of Wales, and was the location of the first university in Wales.

- Aberystwyth was bigger than Cardiff in the seventeenth century, as it was a centre for lead and silver mining from nearby hills and a market town.

- It has a ruined thirteenth-century castle, a pier, a funicular railway and a camera obscura.

- The local weekly paper *The Cambrian News* often reports on the lack of crime with stories such as 'Pie Stolen: police looking for a young man aged 18–21ish wearing blue jeans and a light-colour T-shirt who took a pie from

****

the 24hr Spar'. A particular favourite was 'Nothing stolen from Welsh Water', a headline after the Welsh Water Station was broken into but the interlopers didn't take anything.

LOCAL HEROES

★ The Marxist poet T. E. Nicholas.

★ Gwyn Jones, translator of the *Mabinogion* (a text of Welsh folklore).

★ Mayor Sue Jones-Davies, who played Judith Iscariot in *Monthy Python's Life of Brian*.

★ Malcolm Pryce has written a series of books based around Aberystwyth, the first – *Aberystwyth, Mon Amour* – was serialized on BBC Radio Wales on Sundays at 2 p.m.

★ The Crimea (previously The Crocketts) are a band made of ex-Aberystwyth students.

★ The Might Fuod are an excellent local band.

LLANFAIRPWLLG-WYNGYLLGO-GERYCHWYRND-ROBWLLLLANTYSIL-IOGOGOGOCH

TOASTER: LLIFON WILLIAMS

FAVOURITE FACTS

- Apart from the name we have a column similar to London dedicated to the Marquis of Anglesey, who fought with Nelson. (The Marquis of Anglesey was also one of the first people to have a prosthetic leg.)

- It was the first place in Britain to have a WI meeting.

- Llanfairpwllgwyngyllgogerychwyrndrobwllllantys-iliogogogoch was the password to the headquarters in *Barbarella*.

****

THE MUMBLES, SWANSEA

The Mumbles is a brilliantly named place that has spawned some brilliantly named people. (Paul doesn't mention it here, but are Mumbles dwellers known as Mumblers? Or Mumblies? They ought to be one of those.) First off is vertiginous bassist, lyricist, polemicist and friend of the 6 Music Breakfast Show Nicky Wire. Nicky's name is *allegedly* due to his wiry frame. This also explains Michael Ball's surname.

Another famous Mumbly, according to our Toaster, is Catherine Zeta-Jones. A more delectable vision of womanhood one could never hope to beget, Catherine is, of course, the valley girl who stole the heart of ageing ex-sex addict and actor Michael Douglas. Her name wonderfully combines the commonplace and the cosmic to form something beautifully unusual. Her name is actually completely authentic and not Equity synthesized at all, but would sticking the name of a Greek letter between anyone else's first and second names work as well? Let's have a go . . .

Shaun OMEGA Keaveny
Alf OMICRON Roberts
Sharon XI Shufflebottom
Cyril EPSILON Smith

In short, no.

****

TOASTER: PAUL WHITTAKER

FAVOURITE FACTS

- Catherine Zeta-Jones has a house round the corner, and her dad and Mike Douglas went to the White Rose pub in Mumbles karaoke last year!

$$Z\zeta$$

- Booker Prize-winning author Kingsley Amis lived and taught in Swansea for several years while he brought up his son Martin and wrote the hilarious classic *Lucky Jim* – it was suspected that the university in the book was based on Swansea, but he denied it.

LOCAL HEROES

★ Dylan Thomas drank in The Mumbles and lived in Swansea.

* Nicky Wire and Richie Edwards attended Swansea Uni for three years, and the first Manics gig was in Swansea.

* Paul Newman's daughter married a Mumbles boy, and he was on Caswell beach with the family last summer.

* Bonnie Tyler, Ian Hislop and Rob Brydon are also from around here.

> **SHAUN SEZ:** Nice to see Hislop has retained every nuance of his welsh accent. I once knew a lad whose friends called him Bonnie Tyler, 'cos he was a tiler by trade, and he was fat. You can have that one for nothing.

RHYL

Playlist

▷ **Catatonia** – International Velvet (the song has a line in it which goes 'Darganfyddais gywir baradwys Rhyl', which means 'I discovered the true paradise of Rhyl')

FAVOURITE FACTS

- It was in Rhyl that the infamous egg-throwing attack on John Prescott occurred, during campaigning for the 2001 General Election.

- The Marine Lake used to be a tourist destination, with fairground rides and a zoo. Rhyl Miniature Railway is the only original attraction remaining on the site, a narrow-gauge railway that travels around the lake and is now based at the new museum and railway centre.

LOCAL HEROES

★ Mike Peters of The Alarm.

★ Carol Vorderman

★ Lisa Scott Lee from Steps.

★ Ruth Ellis, the last woman to be hanged in Britain.

****

BARRY

'AN IMPORTANT AND LARGE TOWN'
Barry Town Council website

TOASTER: TOBY

> **Playlist**
>
> ▷ Anything from the **Manics'** album The Holy Bible

FAVOURITE FACTS

- Barry is the setting for BBC 3 hit comedy *Gavin and Stacey*.

- Such is the level of casual menace and miscreance in this wonderful borough that the first 'mosquito' device (the unbearably high-pitched noise inaudible to anyone supposedly over the age of causing mischief) was installed outside a local convenience store.

- The Barry population exploded in the 1890s due to the building of the docks. Now there are pole dancing and burlesque lessons every Thursday at the Wenvoe Arms and there are nine local golf courses. Whether those facts are connected or not I don't know.

- Local Castell Coch was used as Cackle Castle in children's TV series *The Worst Witch*.

- *Doctor Who* episode 'Delta and the Bannermen' was set and filmed in nearby Bannerman. Scenes from episodes 'The Empty Child' and 'The Doctor Dances' were also filmed there.

****

LOCAL HEROES

★ Bryn Merrick, bassist from The Damned.

★ Bob Hope's mum

★ Simon Price, the official Manic Street Preachers biographer.

★ Helen Morgan, former Miss World.

MOLD

TOASTER: HUW

Playlist

▷ **Cable** – Freeze The Atlantic

FAVOURITE FACTS

- There were riots in Mold in 1869 when the English manager of a local coal mine banned speaking Welsh underground. Four people were shot by police and soldiers were drafted in from the nearby city of Chester.

- Mold had the only secret Ministry of Defence site in the UK that was not discovered by German intelligence during the Second World War. The site is still there now (in Rhydymwyn, pronounced 'Rid-Ee-Moo-In') and consists of massive underground chambers in the limestone rock where they used to manufacture and store mustard gas. Grim, I know!

LOCAL HEROES

- ★ Mold and its surrounding villages are home to Rhys Ifans.

- ★ Johnny Buckland (Coldplay guitarist) is from my village home, Pantymwyn (pronounced 'Pan-Tea-Moo-In').

****

TOAST
THE
MIDLANDS

TELFORD

FAVOURITE FACTS

- For a brief period in the late eighties a band from the locality made it big in the UK and in the States. When they were asked to turn on the Christmas lights in this town, the singer less than politely told the council folk where to go.

- Telford is a large new town in the county of Shropshire, approximately 13 miles (21 km) east of Shrewsbury, and 30 miles (48 km) west of Birmingham.

- Telford Shopping Centre is a 50-acre indoor super-regional shopping centre in Telford. It was constructed at the new town's geographical centre, along with an extensive Town Park.

- Basically, Telford is an industrial wasteland that revolves around a huge shopping centre.

- Ironbridge in Telford is a world heritage site. I am unsure what this means, but it's awarded to places like the Taj Mahal and the Pyramids. Maybe so, but to us it's just a left-hand shop.

****

- Roundabouts: we have a lot of roundabouts – possibly the highest ratio of roundabouts to residents in the country.

LOCAL HEROES

★ The poet Philip Larkin worked at a local library. Apparently he was very critical of the town and often complained about it – possibly moaning that he could never get a good kebab.

★ Steve Jones from the band Babybird lived here once. Yes, he goes on about Sheffield and all that, but we have very few people to claim as our own so we will have him.

★ People who have at least at one point called the fair town home include Peter Bengry of Cornershop and Shane Embury of Napalm Death. Local radio station BBC Radio Shropshire also had Chris Hawkins DJing for them.

LINCOLN

One of the great strengths of TTN is the juxtaposition of the mundane and the magnificent. Most Toasts plaster in some spurious Wikipedia-sourced factettes, lace it with a few local legends (did Marlon Brando *really* set fire to his legs with lighter fluid in the toilets of Romford Nando's?), and mention the birthplace of a nationally renowned musician. But a few will include, alongside the usual, a fact so fantastical, so arcane and outlandish, that it is hard to believe. Inspection of James Barron's Toast below leads us to just such a gem. Two in fact. Who knew that the tank, that trusty flattener of wood huts and the hopes of Third World nations everywhere, was actually conceived of IN LINCOLN? As if THAT wasn't unpredictable enough, James follows it with a sucker punch of Ali proportions. According to him, 'Lincoln Cathedral with its original spire, which subsequently fell off, was the first man-made structure constructed to be taller than the Pyramids of Giza' WHAT? REALLY? A cursory check of a few websites beyond our old friend Wiki confirms this to be true.

As aforementioned, this veracity cannot always be assured on TTN. For instance, are we really to believe Chaz in Teddington when he claims that the local Town Hall was designed by Rod Hull? Or Jane from Wincanton's postulation that all four members of Queen stoved in the ground-floor windows of her farmhouse with a hoe whilst singing 'We Are The Champions'? I think not.

Playlist

▷ **Pixies** – Bone Machine (people from the Lincoln and Boston area set up the town of Boston in America, the hometown of The Pixies, in the seventeenth century)

▷ **Supergrass** – Richard III (the brother of Gaz Coombes was in the 22-20s and was the only member not from Lincoln)

▷ **I Was A Cub Scout** – Pink Squares

FAVOURITE FACTS

➤ Lincoln Cathedral was the first man-made structure constructed to be taller than the Pyramids of Giza. However, this was with its original spire, which later fell off.

➤ The first ever tank was invented in Lincoln by William Foster & Co.

➤ The Fosdyke in Lincoln is the country's oldest dyke and it's still in use today. Newport Arch is the only Roman arch in Britain to still be used by traffic.

➤ Lincoln's football team, Lincoln City, were the first team to be automatically relegated from the Football League to the Conference in 1989.

➤ *The Da Vinci Code* movie was filmed at Lincoln Cathedral, doubling for St Paul's Cathedral. One of only four copies of the Magna Carta is stored in Lincoln Castle.

****

- Lincoln was the medieval dyeing capital of Britain, and this is the reason that the colour of Robin Hood's outfit is described as Lincoln Green.

LOCAL HEROES

★ Jim Broadbent, Oscar-winnning actor.

★ Jason Bradbury, presenter of the Channel 5 *Gadget Show*.

★ Jonathan Kerrigan, who used to be in *Heartbeat* and now plays a gay nurse in *Casualty* and *Holby City*.

★ John Hurt went to school in Lincoln.

★ Eamon de Valera, former Irish President, was imprisoned in Lincoln Jail.

★ Alfred Lord Tennyson

★ George Boole, inventor of Boolean algebra, which forms the basis of binary code, making computers possible.

TAMWORTH

TOASTER: NAGSWORTH GOTHERINGTON

> **Playlist**
>
> ▷ **Supergrass** – Caught By The Fuzz (Robert Peel
> did invent the British police force after all)

FAVOURITE FACTS

- Victorian Prime Minister Sir Robert Peel once lived in
  Tamworth. While he was here he bred his own stock of
  pigs with an Irish breed to form the acclaimed Tamworth
  Pig (also known as Sandy Back).

- Tamworth was once the capital of Mercia, Britain's
  largest kingdom.

- Just outside of Tamworth, near Derbyshire, is the
  furthest place in Britain from the sea.

****

- Famous landmarks include the Drayton Manor Theme Park, which had Western Europe's first ever indoor ski slope, located at the Snow Dome.

- In 1345 Tamworth suffered a disastrous fire, and much of the town burned. Fire was a constant hazard in the Middle Ages because most buildings were made of wood with thatched roofs. On the other hand, once burned they could be easily rebuilt.

LOCAL HEROES

★ Julian Cope

★ Iron Maiden's founding member Blaze Bailey came from Tamworth.

BARTON -UPON-HUMBER

'A TOWN WITH A PAST — AND A FUTURE.'
bartonuponhumber.org.uk

Engineering-wise, there are few more impressive and awe-inspiring sights in these British Isles than the Humber Suspension Bridge. Many's the time I have driven underneath it to go to Hull, and I have never failed to be blown away by the audacious spectacle towering above. As a proud Briton, and also a keen devotee of the engineering work of Brunel and his pals, I am angered to the point of punching a puffin that the Golden Gate Bridge gets all the accolades, plaudits, sex and money, whilst the poor old Humber Bridge is left rusting dutifully in the Humber estuary, awash with drizzle, unsung and unloved. Just 'cos the Golden Gate bridge connects to San Francisco, the sun-kissed capital of counter-culture! Well, look, the Humber Bridge is connected to Hull, which has the only white telephone boxes in the country! And BARTON! WHICH HAS A ROPE MUSEUM AND A HAIRY BIKERS' ANNUAL GET-TOGETHER! So put *that* in your pipe and smoke it, San Francisco!

****

Toaster Kirsty below points out the disturbing fact that the suspension bridge is in the red to the tune of £360 million, yet only charges £2.80 per toll bridge use. I am no mathematician but I feel I have come up with a solution. All the bridge owners need to do is increase the toll by, say, £57.20, to £60. Considering 6 million vehicles per year use it, the figure would be paid off in one calendar year! As those annoying meerkats say, SIMPLES!

TOASTER: KIRSTY CHAMP

Playlist

▷ **Cramps** – Creature From Black Leather Lagoon (in honour of bikers and swamp dwellers)

▷ **Motorhead** – Ace Of Spades (for the same reason)

FAVOURITE FACTS

- One of our key attractions is the Humber Bridge, which took eight years to be built and now has a credit-crunching debt of £360 million, from initial estimated cost of £28 million. It costs £2.80 each way for the pleasure of crossing the Humber in a car, to get to Hull and South Yorkshire.

- It also boasts Waters' Edge, one of the UK's greenest buildings, where you can check out your eco-credentials and the innovative CCTV of the wildlife in the nature reserve.

- And then there's the Ropewalk, a gallery and arts and crafts centre that's quarter of a mile long, built to make ropes in 1803 for fishing and whaling vessels and rigging for boats in the Napoleonic wars with France. It also made hemp ropes for Edmund Hillary's Everest climb in 1953.

- On Barton Bike Night every July the town is deluged by bikers for one day. The roads are shut, there are hundreds of bikes, lots of live music and loads of petrolheads. You get to see some great paintwork and amazing customized bikes.

LOCAL HEROES

★ Isaac Pitman, inventor of shorthand.

★ Ken Harrison, Desperate Dan artist.

★ Chad Varah, founder of the Samaritans, was born here (which is ironic, considering the bridge is a key suicide spot).

STRATFORD
-UPON-AVON

TOASTER: TONY 'THE TIGER' HOMER

FAVOURITE FACTS

- We have the only Canada goose control programme outside the USA. It has around 100 resident geese at any one time, but this can rise to 1,000, each depositing about 2lbs of poo every day.

- We have lots of protest groups! BARD (Better Accessible Responsible Development); HOOT (Hands Off Our Theatre); IRATE (Irate Residents Against Tax Excesses); and LOCAL (League of Completely Apathetic Locals), which consists of myself and Geoff. We're totally non-confrontational!

- The British Minigolf Association holds the English Open on the Recreation Ground in Stratford annually. Top player Chris Harding once worked in Waterstone's with me.

- John Harvard, the English clergyman after whom Harvard University is named, came from Stratford.

****

Harvard House in the town is now a museum
and contains a fine collection of pewter.

- George William Childs, American publisher and
  philanthropist, donated a fountain/clock monument
  to the town in 1887 to commemorate Queen Victoria's
  Golden Jubilee. And it's still here!

LOCAL HEROES

★ Michael Ball

★ Anthony Worrall Thompson

★ Simon Gilbert, drummer from Suede (he gave me
  drumming lessons twenty years ago and worked
  in my parents' VG shop in 1980).

Several well-known people also studied here:

★ Gordon Ramsay

★ Simon and Jamie of The Klaxons.

★ Ben Elton

★ Simon Pegg

★ Some writer called William Shakespeare used
  to live round here too.

LOPPINGTON

SPECIAL GUEST TOASTER: BBC 6 MUSIC'S
CHRIS HAWKINS

The village where I was born and grew up boasts a pub, a shop and a church. That's it. There used to be two pubs but one closed due to lack of locals. The population used to be so small, there were only four boys in the village so we had to put my sister in goal for our five-a-side team. It's located in the countryside of North Shropshire and I don't recall anything ever happening. A herd of cows did break through a fence once but only got as far as the churchyard, which meant there was less mowing for the warden to do that summer. Loppington is a little bigger these days and now holds a monthly film club in the refurnished village hall. There are no known connections with celebrity, save the rumour that Ian Hunter (born in nearby Oswestry) once passed through when returning from a Mott The Hoople gig in Wolverhampton. Loppington has probably never been toasted so I hearby raise a glass now.

REDDITCH

Playlist

▷ **The Wonderstuff** – Red Berry Joy Town (my sister seems to think this song may be about Redditch, but I'm not sure)

▷ **Led Zeppelin** – Ramble On (for the unbelievable Jon Bonham drumming)

▷ **Dodgy** – Staying Out For The Summer

FAVOURITE FACTS

➤ Redditch is a new town built to accommodate the overspill from industrial Birmingham.

➤ It has a confusing network of dual carriageways running around it and has the only cloverleaf interchange in Britain.

➤ Redditch became the centre of needle-making from the Middle Ages onwards. Later local industries came to include fish hooks, fishing tackle and later still Royal Enfield motorcycles and Anglepoise lamps.

➤ Supermodel Jodie Kidd moved from London to an eighties semi in Redditch after marrying internet entrepreneur Aidan Butler.

****

- Jacqui Smith used to be a teacher at one of the high schools. She was later the MP for Redditch and eventually became the first female Home Secretary. A friend of mine was sent out of her classroom on local election day for wearing a Conservative rosette. She told him to 'think about what he'd done'.

LOCAL HEROES

★ John Bonham of Led Zepplin was born in Redditch.

★ Rik Mayall spent his early years in Redditch.

★ John Taylor, of Duran Duran fame, went to Abbey High School.

★ Brian Haw, permanent peace protester outside the Houses of Parliament.

★ Mike Cartwright, drummer from infamous Birmingham band The Strawberry Blues, lives in Redditch.

★ Tony Martin, the post-Ozzy Osbourne Black Sabbath singer, named the *Headless Cross* album after a district in Redditch.

★ The actress who plays the blonde girl in *Hollyoaks* who had an affair with an older man lives here.

HEREFORD

Playlist

▷ **John Lee Hooker** – Boom Boom (because of the Blues Brothers connection through Frank Oz)

▷ **The Pretenders** – Message Of Love (they are from Hereford)

▷ **Talking Heads** – Road To Nowhere

FAVOURITE FACTS

- The name 'Hereford' is said to come from the Anglo-Saxon 'here', an army or formation of soldiers, and 'ford', a place for crossing a river. We're a little county tucked away on the Welsh border which some maps still refer to by the legend 'There Be Dragons'.

- Hereford was founded in around AD 700 and became the Saxon capital of West Mercia. It was the focal point for repelling Welsh attacks.

- Hereford is a wasteland for live music as there's no decent venue, but I have seen the likes of Pulp and Jethro Tull play the local leisure centre. Hawkwind turned up to headline a small festival last year (but let's face it, Hereford must be one of the few places they haven't played before in the last thirty-five years), and,

****

rather bizarrely, I recently found Mick Jagger's brother Chris playing in a local Jazz Café.

- The Mappa Mundi, a thirteenth-century A–Z of the world, is housed in Hereford Cathedral, which itself dates back to the tenth century. It's supposed to be magnificent, but I've never been arsed to visit it. Apparently it's wrong anyway: Africa and Asia are labelled backwards, Jerusalem is in the middle, east is up, and England and Ireland are in the bottom left.

- Hereford's obscurity was finally brought to the world's attention when Robert de Niro mentioned Hereford to expose Sean Bean as a fraud in *Ronin*. The town is in fact so obscure that none of the road signs mention it until you are basically in town.

LOCAL HEROES

★ The Pretenders (pre-Chrissie Hynde) hailed from Hereford.

★ Mott the Hoople – Pete Overend Watts used to run a Ye Olde Curiosity Shop in the city.

★ Frank Oz, best known for performing with Jim Henson's Muppets, was born here. His characters included Miss Piggy, Fozzie Bear, Animal and Sam the Eagle on *The Muppet Show*, and Grover, Cookie Monster and Bert on *Sesame Street*, among many others. He briefly appeared in *The Blues Brothers* as the correction officer handing back Jon Belushi his property upon his release from jail with the words: 'One unused prophylactic . . . one soiled.'

CORBY

To me, an exiled northerner-down-south, damned forever to a purgatory of frustrating motorway navigation, Corby is one of 'those' places. A hinterland, an unknown quantity, a name without a face. A place whose name one whistles past at 70 miles per hour on the M1 on the way to somewhere more personally significant whilst one's thoughts turn to Ginsters, coffee and urinary relief. Of course, Corby also brings to mind the eponymous, universally experienced but seldom-used trouser press. One cannot help but think that whoever had the initial job of selling the Corby trouser press perhaps rustled up a ruse involving a drunken night of revelry with the nation's hotel managers, a donkey, a prostitute, a Polaroid camera and little left to the imagination. Short of pure bribery, how else could so many hotels have been coerced into purchasing a contraption that has pressed so few trousers?

What puts the 'COR!' in Corby, then? You will see below that our Corby Toaster found much to recommend it, including a visit from *Coronation Street's* Brian Tilsley (apparently it was like when the Pope went to Liverpool, but with more signed breasts), an original member of party pop purveyors Paper Lace and the regular appearance of the diminutive Don Estelle on the local bandstand . . . take it away, ROB WALDREN . . .

TOASTER: ROB WALDREN

Playlist

▷ **The Specials** – Ghost Town

▷ **St Cecilia** – Leap Up And Down (Wave Your Knickers In The Air)

▷ **Paper Lace** – Billy Don't Be A Hero

▷ Anything by **Raging Speedhorn**

FAVOURITE FACTS

- Corby is in Northants in the Midlands but has a large Scottish population.

- It used to be a big steel town, but the steel works closed and everyone got drunk for a few decades. But now it's on the rise again – it has its own Primark now, and we are going to have a train station in a few months!

- There is a highland gathering every year, and famous people come to it. One year it was Brian Tilsley from *Coronation Street*.

- They used to have a recurring event where the very small man from *It Ain't Half Hot Mum* would sing on the bandstand up town accompanied by an organist and dressed in the *It Ain't Half Hot Mum* gear.

LOCAL HEROES

★ Johnny Vaughan was said to have lived here at some point. It's rumoured he was a lifeguard for a bit at the Corby swimming pool.

★ Bill Drummond from KLF.

★ Raging Speedhorn, a quite famous band, hail from Corby.

★ John Proctor of St Cecilia lives in Corby. They were famous for a number one in the seventies called 'Leap Up And Down (Wave Your Knickers In The Air)'. He now works as an IT teacher in the town.

★ My mum's boyfriend was in an early incarnation of Paper Lace before they got famous with 'Billy Don't Be A Hero'. And his name is Billy!

★ Andrew Cowan is Corby's most famous writer. He wrote a book based in Corby called *Pig* and was showered with awards for it, winning the Betty Trask Award, the *Sunday Times* Young Writer of the Year Award, a Scottish Arts Council Book Award and the Ruth Hadden Memorial Award.

★ The lead singer from Shawaddywaddy also lives just outside Corby and can be seen shopping in our local Asda.

NORTHAMPTON

Every town has a talking point. Whether it's Norris the Homeless Clown Busker, the controversial proposed bus-station refurb or the disgraced lottery millionaire's bankruptcy trial, these are the touchstones that bring all the townsfolk together in a tapestry of tittle-tattle and trivia. Another great talking point for many is the Highest Point. Some lucky conurbations may count a delightful eleventh-century cathedral as theirs, others, the headquarters of a multinational company, but others still are somewhat less impressive. In Leigh, my home town, it was the BICC Tower, a skyline-besmirching concrete hammer looming over the centre that, folklore whispered, swayed up to a metre in each direction in high winds. Now it has been dismantled many Leithers still look back fondly on what they call 'our Empire State'. According to Toaster Damien Smith of Northampton, theirs is the Express Lift Tower, the only purpose-built lift-testing centre in the UK. What few people know is that, in a nod of deference to this monolith of lift technology, all lifts built in the UK are fitted facing the Northampton Express Lift Tower, the Mecca of Lifts.

TOASTER: DAMIEN SMITH

Playlist

▷ **Patrick Macnee and Honor Blackman** – Kinky Boots (tooooo obvious)

▷ **Spacemen 3** – Walking With Jesus

▷ **Spiritualized** – Run

FAVOURITE FACTS

- Northampton is famous for its shoe industry. Three main companies still dominate: Church's, Loake (by appointment to HRH) and Tricker's, which is famous for being used in the film *Kinky Boots*.

- We have a Carlsberg brewery in the town – doesn't make it any cheaper to drink here, though.

- The Express Lift Tower dominates the skyline. Wogan refers to it as the 'Lighthouse of Northampton'. Commissioned in 1978 and opened in 1982, it was the only purpose-built lift-testing tower in UK. It's now grade 2 listed, and we believe it's still the youngest listed building in the UK.

LOCAL HEROES

★ Des O'Connor was originally from East London but was evacuated to Northampton during the Second World War.

★ Alan Carr grew up in Northampton, with his dad famously being the Northampton FC manager.

****

★ Andrew Collins is Northampton through and through and did well locally with his book *Where Did It All Go Right?*

> **SHAUN SEZ:** Collins is one of the many greats I have been lucky enough to work alongside at 6 Music. I have admired his work, it seems, since the dawn of time. He looks about my age, though he seems to have been in the public eye forever. Which either means that he has discovered the secret of agelessness, or that his career began when he was aged six.

★ Alan Moore was born in the town. He's famous not only as the greatest graphic novelist of all time (*From Hell*, *V for Vendetta*, *Watchmen* and many others) but also for refusing to accept money for the films of his books, which he doesn't even want to see.

★ Malcolm Arnold, composer, conductor and all-round good guy. He's perhaps best known maybe for writing the music for *The Bridge on the River Kwai* as well as conducting the Royal Philharmonic on Deep Purple's *Live at the Royal Albert Hall* LP.

★ Jon Mattock, the drummer from Spacemen 3, hailed from Northampton. He was also in Spiritualized, and I think he still works at the local college in something to do with music production.

BIRMINGHAM

TOASTERS: FLO BETTS
JON BOUNDS

Playlist

▷ **Black Sabbath** – Iron Man (Ozzy is a famous son of Birmingham. We have an Iron Man statue in Victoria Square by artist Antony Gormley, and it's a tip of the hat to our industrial heritage)

▷ **Spencer Davies Group** – Keep On Running (they were formed in Birmingham in 1963)

▷ **Dexys Midnight Runners** – Gino (Kevin Rowland founded the band in Birmingham in 1978, although he is originally from Wolverhampton. But I think we can forgive him that)

▷ **ELO** – Mr Blue Sky (it's played before Birmingham City come out to play)

FAVOURITE FACTS

- The world's first Odeon cinema opened in Birmingham in 1930.

- Britain's first ever four-wheel petrol-driven car was made in the city by Frederick Lanchester in 1895.

****

- Custard powder was invented in Birmingham in 1837 by Alfred Bird (who was by profession a pharmacist). The original custard factory is now a popular arts venue and night spot, imaginatively called The Custard Factory.

- Birmingham now has a 'walk of fame' just like Hollywood. We've placed stars for Ozzy, Noddy Holder and Jasper Carrot so far. Benny out of *Crossroads* can't be far behind.

LOCAL HEROES

★ Bill Oddie

★ J. R. R. Tolkien – legend has it he wrote *The Hobbit* in an area called Moseley Bog. It is a natural bog on some grassland in a Birmingham suburb – not a public toilet.

★ Tony Hancock

★ Ozzy Osbourne

★ Barbara Cartland

★ Neville 'Peace in our time' Chamberlain.

★ Murray Walker

★ Noddy Holder

★ Frank Skinner

LICHFIELD

Playlist

▷ **TV On The Radio** – Golden Age (because it's from the album *Dear Science!*)

FAVOURITE FACTS

- Lichfield has the only three-spired cathedral in the country. It was established by St Chad in 669.

- Edward Wightman was the last person to be burned at the stake for heresy, and it was done in Lichfield!

- The first dictionary was written in Lichfield by its most famous resident, Samuel Johnson, who's just celebrated his 300th birthday!

LOCAL HEROES

★ During the eighteenth century it became a centre of great intellectual activity, and, aside from the great Doctor Johnson, other residents included David Garrick (who helped popularize Shakespeare in the eighteenth century), Erasmus Darwin (grandfather of Charles and a great scientist and poet in his own right) and Anna Seward (the poet known as the Swan of Lichfield).

★ A more recent resident is Helen Baxendale from *Cold Feet* and *Friends* (who used to go to my old school).

★ Richard Allinson (Radio 2).

★ Richie Edwards – he took over from the other guy who played bass for The Darkness.

THE POTTERIES

TOASTER: LIZA O'CONNOR

Playlist

▷ **Iggy Pop** – Lust For Life

FAVOURITE FACTS

- The local bus service was called the PMT (Potteries Motor Traction), and, yes, all the buses were bright red – used to amuse me hugely when I was kid.

- You can always spot an ex-resident of Stoke in a restaurant: they are the one looking at the underside of the plate to see where it's made.

- Obviously we're also home to the once-thriving pottery industry – it has more Doulton figures per square inch than anywhere else in the world.

LOCAL HEROES

★ Famous Stokeys include Sir Stanley Matthews, Robbie Williams, Anthea Turner, Nick Hancock, Neil Morrissey.

★ We've got a strong rock heritage too: Slash from Guns 'n' Roses lived here as a child, and Lemmy of Motorhead was born in Stoke-on-Trent.

★ Plus the captain of the *Titanic*, Edward John Smith, was from here too.

****

NUNEATON

Nuneaton is dealt with beautifully here in a quintessential Toast courtesy of local resident Claudia. Here, as with all great Toasts, fact and folklore ride the same horse. We can ascertain through public record that seventies primetime favourite Larry Grayson (a much underrated comic as far as I am concerned by the way) indeed came from the town. A map can easily show that the inappropriately named Nuneaton ring-road actually goes *through* Nuneaton as opposed to *around* it. (I'd be nervous of having a heart-bypass in Nuneaton General if this is the way they go about things.) But the most tantalizing, piquant and probably untrue 'fact' here is the one about Macca (Lord Thumbs, Frog Meister General) buying flowers from a local florist in the town. Much as we would love to believe it, it must be filed alongside those other Beatles myths, such as the 'Paul is dead' story of 1967, that 'Lucy In The Sky With Diamonds' was a song specifically about LSD, or the one that suggests Paul McCartney wrote some good songs after 1983. *(Actually, Shaun, that is harsh. 'My Brave Face' was excellent, and there have been moments of inspiration along the way. Have I spoiled your paragraph? Sorry. Ed)*

On a different, bum note, the choice of song here, 'My Generation', reminds me of the very first full band practice my now-legendary and massively influential band Mosque had back in the tail end of 1987. (If the name doesn't ring an immediate bell, 1: CALL YOURSELF A MUSIC FAN? and 2: google 'Mosque: most underrated band in history'.) After months of looking for a suitable sticksman to be the powerhouse behind our revolutionary post-punk noise, we finally found one in the unusual shape of Eddie. Being the purists that we were, and wishing to preserve the unique musical unity and telepathy we had nurtured in our first explosive meetings, we were delighted to finally find a drummer who met our hugely exacting specifications, i.e. one who had his own kit and a dad who could drop him off at practices.

As we'd never played with a drummer before (neither had Kate Moss at this time, unbelievably), the anticipation and sheer excitement in the air upstairs at the Three Crowns Hotel and Pub was palpable. I can only imagine it was much the same as the feeling in the room at St Peter's Church Hall in Woolton in 1959 when a young McCartney and Lennon met for the first time. As Eddie's father's black Range Rover pulled into the car park, our collective hearts skipped as we glanced, on the back seats, a huge seven-piece black Pearl Export kit! Eddie leaped out of the front seat and immediately looked the part. Like a young and handsome Tom Cruise, he wore a black leather jacket, jeans, white T-shirt and *even* black fingerless drumming gloves. 'My GOD!' we thought. 'THE GUY IS A DRUMMING LEGEND!'

Hurriedly we collected the drums and helped Eddie set them up. Soon Eddie was seated behind his vast black instrument, exuding ineffable cool and confidence. 'So what do you guys wanna play?' said Eddie nonchalantly. At this point, our mood had shifted from one of excitement to one of intimidation. How could we be fit to so much as polish the drumstool of this percussive panacea? We collectively gulped, steeled ourselves and called out, '"My Generation" by The Who.'

What could be a more perfect shop window for the adventurous, animalistic yet artful drumming Eddie was clearly capable of? 'No worries,' he offered. Banksy, the bass player, counted us in. 'All in at the top, remember, ONE-TWO-THREE-FOUR!'

It's difficult to describe Eddie's sound, or 'vibe', using just words. Some said it sounded like a hundred oil drums cascading down Leigh's Town Hall steps. Others said it sounded like a one-man band being dropped out of a helicopter into a jewellery shop. I still maintain it sounded like someone building a shed. He was not so much Cozy Powell as Peter Powell. Less Moon, more Uranus. Needless to say, poor Eddie, despite his big kit, became the victim of Mosque's first ruthless sacking. It was certainly not to be the last. (To read more about Mosque, check out the upcoming biography *Shoes off Please! The Official Story of Mosque*, by Paul Morley.)

TOASTER: CLAUDIA FORSTER

Playlist

▷ **The Who** – My Generation (Larry Grayson used to present *The Generation Game*)

****

FAVOURITE FACTS

- Nuneaton is the largest town in Warwickshire, and locally reared George Eliot gave a thinly veiled portrait of it in her first work of fiction, *Scenes of Clerical Life* (1858).

- For some reason the Nuneaton ring-road runs through the centre of the town! (So, not much of a ring-road...)

- The house that Mary Whitehouse used to live in in the town is now a sex shop!

- We don't get many famous people round here. The best I can do is that there's a rumour Paul McCartney once bought a bunch of flowers from a local florist.

> **SHAUN SEZ:** I tried to come up with some flower/ Macca song-related punnery to insert here but couldn't! If YOU have one, please send it to me on a stamped-addressed envelope to the following address: 'SHAUN KEAVENY, LONDON'. That should get to me.

LOCAL HEROES

- ★ George Eliot (Mary Ann Evans)
- ★ Ken Loach
- ★ Larry Grayson
- ★ Mary Whitehouse

NEWCASTLE -UNDER- LYME

TOASTER: KEVIN WINDSOR

Playlist

▷ **Ting Tings** – That's Not My Name

FAVOURITE FACTS

- Newcastle-under-Lyme is part of a worldwide network of towns and cities with the name Newcastle.

- The annual Newcastles of the World Summit was held in Newcastle-under-Lyme for six days from 17 June 2006.

- When Stoke-on-Trent was formed by the 1910 amalgamation of the 'six towns' (Stoke, Hanley, Fenton, Longton, Burslem and Tunstall), Newcastle remained separate.

WELLINGBOROUGH

TOASTER: ALAN PRICE

Playlist

▷ **Bauhaus** – Ziggy Stardust

FAVOURITE FACTS

➤ To commemorate the fact that Oliver Cromwell stayed in the Hind Hotel the night before the Battle of Naseby, we have the annual Battle of the Shopping Trolleys (sponsored by Matalan) in the hotel's car park. The fight takes place between two teams of teenagers – one to represent the Cavaliers, the other the Roundheads.

➤ Wellingborough had a zoo from 1943 to 1970. When it was demolished, the Borough Council offices were built on the site, which we thought was very appropriate.

****

- Wellingborough has had a very strong Polish connection since the Second World War. The Polish population of the town is now some 5 per cent of the total; we have Polish shops, clubs and other amenities. Other initiatives under consideration include permitting the Polish Road Traffic Authority to open a special window at the main post office for Poles to tax their cars; and compulsory Polish lessons in schools for all five- to seven-year-olds.

LOCAL HEROES

★ Bauhaus's Pete Murphy was brought up in Wellingborough, as well as Radiohead's Thom Yorke.

★ Sir David Frost attended Wellingborough Grammar School.

ILKESTON

TOASTER: KIRK BRADSHAW

> **Playlist**
>
> ▷ **Eels** – Railroad Man

FAVOURITE FACTS

- We have had a fair, granted by Royal Charter, since the year 1252, and every October for one week we get overrun with travelling fairground 'pikeys' and their unsafe and extortionately priced rides. It's wonderful.

- Ilkeston is often locally spelt Ilson, as it's pronounced in the local tongue, which is East Midlands English and apparently spoken in only a few areas. We're good at making a whole sentence sound as one word!

****

- Ilson was probably founded in the sixth century AD. It appears in the Domesday Book as Tilchestune. It used to have three train stations but now has none. They talk of a new one, but it's hollow words.

- The local wrought-iron viaduct (Bennerley Viaduct) is a grade 2 listed building and stands in its entirety even though the banks have been removed either end, making it look a little weird; it's known as the forgotten bridge (so my dad says).

LOCAL HEROES

★ D. H. Lawrence – some of his characters were written speaking the Ilson dialect because he lived quite locally at one point.

★ Robert Lindsay was born here, and his dad still lives here.

COLESHILL

'VERY MUCH A TOWN OF THE PRESENT'
Official website

I often dream entire fictional ad campaigns. Recently I dreamed a fantastic idea for an advert for stock cubes. In short, it involved ubiquitous salad-peddling mockney Jamie Oliver and a set of medieval stocks. (I know some of you can already see where I'm going with this.) Jamie was locked in the stocks and in the first commercial bombarded with a barrage of frozen chickens. After ten seconds of this, the voiceover said, 'Chicken stock. While stocks last,' and the process was repeated for vegetable and fish stocks. I am sure you will agree that, if I were to take this idea to any top-line advertising agency such as Saatchi, they would not only snatch my hand off for it, but offer me a job as a senior ad exec on the spot.

This neatly brings us to Stuart's Toast of Coleshill (sorry Coes-ill – why-oh-WHY don't people spell it like we say it?). It contains the fact that the town houses Warwickshire's only stocks, used for punishing drunks and 'bakers who sold underweight loaves'. We certainly have moved on as a society, haven't we? That said, perhaps if we *did* lock booze-bingeing teens up in the stocks of a Saturday night and let *Daily Mail* readers fling festering fruit at them, the world *might* become a better place? (That was a blatant attempt to curry favour with the editor of said newspaper in the hope they might give me a column.)

Speaking of bakers in stocks, there is one I would very much like to subject to such punishment. I recently went

****

to a national department store's food hall and purchased what *looked* like a perfectly harmless loaf of rustic rye bread for dietary reasons I shall not bore you with. When I got home and checked my receipt, I realized I had been charged (I suggest those of a tightarsed persuasion sit down at this point, preferably with a brown paper bag at the ready to breathe into) FOUR POUNDS FIFTY for it! FOUR POUNDS FIFTY FOR A LOAF OF BREAD! And NO, it was NOT four feet long. At that price I felt unjustified in eating it all at once, so for the last six months I have been slicing a piece off, freezing it, thawing it out a week later, slicing another piece, and refreezing. At least now I feel I have got my money's worth.

TOASTER: STUART HARRISON

Playlist

▷ **Adam And The Ants** – Stand And Deliver
(due to Coleshill's coaching history)

FAVOURITE FACTS

- Coleshill is pronounced *coes-ill* with no 'l' or 'h'. It's had settlers for thousands of years – a local Roman site was excavated in the 1980s.

- Coleshill School is one of oldest in the country, founded in 1520.

****

- Coleshill houses Warwickshire's only stocks including pillory and whipping post for drunks and bakers who sold underweight loaves.

LOCAL HEROES

★ Author George Eliot was born in Coleshill, as was Sherlock Holmes actor Jeremy Brett.

★ Local cinema owner John Wynn was caught transmitting information to the Germans during the Second World war. So not so much of a hero, then.

NOTTINGHAM

TOASTER: GEORGINA

Playlist

▷ **The Rifles** – Robin Hood

FAVOURITE FACTS

- There are three pubs in Nottingham that all claim to be 'England's Oldest Pub'.

- The city is home to the Screen cinema, which claims to be world's smallest cinema with only twenty-one seats.

- Quentin Tarantino held the première of *Reservoir Dogs* at the Broadway cinema in Nottingham in 1992.

- Nottingham has won the 'Britain in Bloom' competition several times.

LOCAL HEROES

- ★ Robin Hood, obviously.

- ★ Dale Winton is well known in Nottingham for his stint on Radio Trent.

- ★ Torville and Dean

- ★ The lead guitarist from Editors, and the drummer from Deep Purple.

- ★ John Boot, the founder of Boots, D. H. Lawrence and Su Pollard are also from Nottingham.

****

ASHBY-DE-LA-ZOUCH

TOASTER: JOE ASKEW

Playlist

▷ **The Young Knives** – Up All Night

FAVOURITE FACTS

- Aside from its exotic name, Ashby is the home of delicious KP snacks (other savoury snacks are available!). They make hula hoops, skips, peanuts and chocdips – remember them? I've got friends who still work at KP. Apparently there's a discount shop at the factory where you can buy misformed KP products, like skips that haven't swollen properly – yum!

- Ashby is the furthest town away from the sea in the UK.

LOCAL HEROES

★ The Young Knives

****

MOUNTSORREL

If there is any point whatsoever to this Toasting of the Nation, it is that even the most insignificant of local facts should be proudly boasted and celebrated. George, here toasting the sublimely named town of Mountsorrel, rightly feels no embarrassment in telling us that 'An actress who played a member of the Dingle family in one episode of *Emmerdale* lives up my road!' We know not who. We have no character or actress name. But that is less important than the fact that George has encapsulated that brief frisson of excitement one feels when one finds that one is living adjacent to a TV star. Indeed, it is fair to say that this unidentified actress's star burned briefly, like a brilliant boulder of heavenly rock disintegrating in the atmosphere, but her stardust scattered down and alighted on everyone in her locale.

As if that wasn't enough excitement for one town, George then, almost carelessly, tosses in one final match to the tinderbox of excitement, by imparting that none other than nineties leotard-donning fitness guru Rosemary Conley used to live in Mountsorrel before relocating to nearby Quorn. It is not suggested that she did so to be closer to the origin of the meat-substitute of the same name, but surely that's a likely motive. I cannot believe for a moment that a woman as dedicated to personal wellbeing and fitness as Rosemary would for a moment consider moving to Pie Town New Mexico, or for that matter Madras in India.

Finally, on the subject of Quorn, I was recently flabbergasted to discover that one of England's oldest hunts is the Quorn Hunt! OH THE IRONY! The name evokes a wonderful image of red-coated men on horseback, blaring horns and rousing dogs in wild chase of a box of veggie sausages being dragged through a field by a jeep. Less cruel than killing a fox, and much more delicious with ketchup. WIN WIN!

TOASTER: GEORGE OVERTON

Playlist

▷ **Elvis Presley** – Shake, Rattle And Roll

SHAUN SEZ: My little boy, Arthur, is totally obsessed with the King. Naturally I began the indoctrination, but he now demands I play him the 68 Comeback Special, and can even do the 'ahu-huh!' impression on demand. Props to the kid!

FAVOURITE FACTS

➤ Mountsorrel's got the biggest granite quarry in Europe in it, which blasts at 12.30 every weekday with a force you can feel all over the village. A steam train used to run from the quarry to the historic Great Central Railway, which runs nearby. I'm currently involved in a project to bring some of that railway line back into use.

****

- The Grand Union Canal runs through the village, and there used to be a castle on top of the hill here.

- An actress who played a member of the Dingle family in one episode of *Emmerdale* lives up my road!

- Felix Buxton from Basement Jaxx went to nearby Loughborough Grammar School.

LOCAL HEROES

★ No local heroes live in the village as such. Rosemary Conley, the health and fitness guru, used to live here. But she moved next door to Quorn.

DERBY

'A CITY FOR ALL AGES'
Official website

There is a fond melancholy in Miles's Toast of Derby. The facts are shot through with self-deprecating smallness. From the musical reference (Miles chose White Town as it's 'Derby's only number one') to the tragedy that is Derby's bulldozed bus station, Miles paints a picture of a slightly under-achieving town, beset by problems of its own making. Then, at the end, just as you think you know all there is to know about this small Anytown in Midlandville, Britain, he SMACKS you up with the *incredible* fact that 40 PER CENT OF THE WORLD'S CHRISTMAS PUDDINGS come from Derby! IN YOUR FACE, MELTON MOWBRAY! I BET YOU'D KILL FOR THAT KIND OF MARKET SHARE WITH YOUR PORK PIES!

But there is a darker side to Derby not mentioned by Miles, perhaps understandably. Through exhaustive research (Google) I obtained this information from a BBC Derby website: 'the annoying novelty tune "Agadoo" was supposedly recorded by Black Lace after hearing the French original during a night out at "Gossips", one of Derby's most popular nightclubs of the eighties.' In essence, this is the smoking gun. It now seems certain that, were it not for Derby's Gossips nightclub, Britain would never have had to endure the lasting horror of this monster 1984 hit for Black Lace, the reverberations of which have been felt through time. What is, for me, most shocking, is the fact that the song was a cover version, originally recorded in 1971 by Michel Delancray and Mya Symille. It

****

puts me in mind of US President Woodrow Wilson's quote of 1917, describing the First World War as 'The war to end all wars'. He was, of course, hopelessly naive. Despite the horror of that conflict, it has not dampened man's desire to destroy. History, it seems, never learns its lesson. How else can you explain the unexplainable? That two men sporting bleach-blond Limahl spiky hair and Hawaiian shirts could venture into a Midlands nightclub, hear 'Agadoo' and think, 'More people need to hear this song!' To see it happen once is atrocious. Twice, an atrocity. Derby, hang your head in shame for your part.

TOASTER: MILES TEBUTT

Playlist

▷ **White Town** – Your Woman
(Derby's only number one single)

SHAUN SEZ: This song holds haunting memories of 1996, when I was working for a Manchester temping agency on floor 15 of an office block in the city centre. Sometimes I still look back with fondness at those long afternoons I spent being shouted at by pensioners. It's also entirely true that one of my customers' surnames was TWATT. Classic!

FAVOURITE FACTS

- Derby is the only city in the UK without a bus station, after the council bulldozed the old one then never built another.

- Ghost war: according to local historian Richard Felix (an expert on *Most Haunted*), Derby is the most haunted city in the UK. This quite upset York, which had always laid claim to this status.

- The world's biggest ever bowl of popcorn was prepared at UCI cinema at the Meteor Centre in 1991. It took staff from the cinema three days to complete the record, starting on 23 August and finishing on 26 August.

LOCAL HEROES

★ Matthew Walker – set up a Christmas pudding factory in Derby in 1899. Now 40 per cent of all Christmas puddings eaten in the world are Matthew Walker ones!

SHREWSBURY

TOASTER: AMY TAYLOR

> **Playlist**
>
> ▷ **Fatboy Slim** – Right Here, Right Now (connection with Charles Darwin – in the video, a monkey evolves into a man from the cover of the *You've Come A Long Way Baby* album)

FAVOURITE FACTS

- Shrewsbury is the unlikely home to the world's first skyscraper. Ditherington flax mill, built in 1797, was the first multi-storey iron-framed building ever built, and therefore the forerunner of every skyscraper and tower block in the world.

- In the graveyard of St Chad's Church in Shrewsbury lies the grave of Ebenezer Scrooge – the 1984 film *A Christmas Carol*, starring George C. Scott, used Shrewsbury as a location, and after the film crew left, the grave remained.

- Even the local residents can't agree on how to pronounce Shrewsbury. Some people prefer the historical Shrowsbury (rhymes with 'throw'), while others prefer Shrewsbury (to rhyme with 'threw'). There is no official pronunciation, so you can take your pick.

- There's a street in Shrewsbury called Grope Lane, which is where ladies of the night operated in the sixteenth century.

****

Many other cites had Grope Lanes as well, but most of them have since been renamed to the more innocent-sounding Grape Lane or Grove Lane.

- The Brother Cadfael novels by Ellis Peters are set in Shrewsbury Abbey, but the TV series starring Derek Jacobi was filmed in Hungary because Shrewsbury doesn't look medieval any more!

LOCAL HEROES

★ Alumni from Shrewsbury School include John Peel, Michael Palin, Nick Hancock and Michael Heseltine.

★ Charles Darwin was born in Shrewsbury at his family home, the Mount, in 1809 and was also educated at Shrewsbury School.

TOAST

NORTH OF

ENGLAND

LEEDS

Leeds, as more than one Toaster has helped show over the years, is awash with historical significance, civic charm and depth of character. For instance, would the average placid casual know that moving-picture technology, which has subsequently given rise to everything from *Citizen Kane* to *Surprise Surprise*, first flickered into life on a Leeds back wall? Or that that most quintessentially British of institutions Marks and Spencer was founded in Leeds as a penny bazaar back in 1884? Probably not. But to me, that's not what Leeds really means.

That's because I served my time at the coal face of higher education at Leeds Trinity All Saints College. Due to three years of squalor, Third World levels of deprivation and herculean imbibing of inadvisable quantities of White Lightning, I have few memories of Leeds beyond having stones thrown at me by local children as I waited for a bus, seeing the next-door neighbour's front door being kicked in by a drug dealer whilst we watched *EastEnders* and eating chilli-con-carne pizzas from the local Co-Op. I realize that this is not typical of the Leeds experience, rather a depressing snapshot of life on a shoestring in early-nineties Headingley, but nonetheless these are my recollections. For a more rounded view of the delights and nuances of Leeds living, please see below.

TOASTERS: JOHN JAMES
         DOM HIGGINS
         JACK

Playlist

▷ **Kaiser Chiefs** – Every Day I Love You Less And Less

▷ **The Wedding Present** – Everyone Thinks He Looks Daft

▷ **Ash** – Shining Light
  (for Matthew Hoggard – Ashes winner!)

FAVOURITE FACTS

- Leeds was once called Loidis, and was recorded as early as AD 731 in Bede's *History of the English Church and People*.

- Louis le Prince used a Leeds back garden as his subject for the first ever moving images in October 1880.

- The Lumiere Building Development in the city centre is going to be the tallest residential development in Europe. It is currently the shortest, however, as they ran out of funding when the credit crunch hit. Only the foundations had been put in, so it's just a hole in the ground for now!

- Michael Marks opened his Penny Bazaar at Kirkgate Market here in 1884. This was to lead ultimately to the foundation of Marks and Spencer in 1890.

- It's twinned with eight cities, including Colombo (Sri Lanka) and Durban (South Africa).

- Leeds is the new home of the resurgent Northern Soul movement, shifting from Wigan, which was apparently the hub in the seventies and eighties (so I'm told by my dad!).

****

- Royston Langdon, the lead singer from Spacehog, allegedly used to live in Headingley with his now estranged wife, Liv Tyler. She is said to be a member of a working men's club in the city.

- Leeds' West Indian Carnival in Chapeltown is the longest-running West Indian carnival in Europe (1967).

LOCAL HEROES

- ★ Peter O'Toole

- ★ Alan Bennett

- ★ Julian Barratt (of The Mighty Boosh).

- ★ John Craven

- ★ Jeremy Paxman

- ★ Ernie Wise

- ★ John Smeaton, the father of civil engineering.

- ★ Vic Reeves

- ★ Nell McAndrew

- ★ Jimmy Savile

- ★ Mel B

- ★ Matthew Hoggard

- ★ Chris Moyles

- ★ Bands: Sisters Of Mercy, Haggis Horns, Soft Cell, Chumbawumba, Kaiser Chiefs, Corinne Bailey-Rae, Pigeon Detectives.

****

NORTON

Many of our Toasters share an innate sense of sanguinity in the face of failure, and this is shown to great effect in Alan Brown's entry below. Much like Toaster Margaret O'Hare, whose first fact about Belfast (see p.270) is that it built the *Titanic*, Alan hits us with the impressive fact that the first bell for Big Ben's clock tower was cast in his home town of Norton, only to tell us in the next breath that it broke in transit to London. The opening credits to *News at Ten* must sound like a hollow ringing mockery to the people of Norton, their moment of bell-based glory forever dashed on the vicious rocks of fate.

Here, though, we also see the potentially ugly, even aggressive side that Toast the Nation can unleash in an otherwise temperate person. Further down the Toast we see that Alan says Norton has the only Anglo-Saxon church in the north – St Mary's. He closes with a goading 'Top that, Bolton!' Despite my best efforts to keep this a tome that represents unity, charity, hope and optimism, I can see more and more that, in fact, it could easily become the catalyst for the first civil war this country has seen in centuries. If we aren't watchful, people could read this book, become enraged by the claims of people in rival towns and take to the streets with makeshift weapons, eager to defend their town's claim on the smallest pub, narrowest ginnel or oldest Anglo-Saxon church. If you, or anyone you know, feel you may be close to organizing an armed militia or uprising as a result of reading this book, may I please implore you to STEP BACK FROM THE MADNESS. Count to ten, have a cup of tea and watch *Countdown*.

****

TOASTER: ALAN BROWN

Playlist

▷ **Lemon Jelly** – Nice Weather For Ducks (we've got a top duck pond)

FAVOURITE FACTS

- Norton dates back to Anglo-Saxon times – it has the only Anglo-Saxon church in the north – St Mary's. Top that, Bolton!

- The first bell for Big Ben was cast here, but it broke on the way down to London.

- The world's first train ticket was bought in nearby Stockton.

LOCAL HEROES

★ Film director Franc Roddam (*Quadrophenia*) was born here.

★ Duncan Bannatyne from *Dragons' Den* was married in the church and has bought a house in Norton.

> **SHAUN SEZ:** He spends most of his time in his house in the South of France though. So for that reason, he's out.

****

* Stephen Tompkinson (*Drop the Dead Donkey*) and Richard Griffiths (Monty in *Withnail and I*) are both from nearby Stockton.

* John Walker, inventor of the match in 1826, is buried here.

> **SHAUN SEZ:** It says on his tombstone: 'In death, he met his match.' (It doesn't really.)

HULME

Hulme. Much like Wolverhampton or Scunthorpe, it's a town with a name that's difficult to love. It conjures images of high-rise flats, town-planning aberrations and greyness. So it was a surprise to me when Toaster of the area Joe Marshall claimed that one of the coolest musicians on the planet, The Velvet Underground's Nico, had a flat there back in the day – wow! Imagine popping to the shop for a Wispa and a bottle of milk only to see Andy Warhol's muse and Lou Reed's lover in the queue holding a *TV Quick*! Actually that reminds me of the time I saw Prince, complete with twenty-two-strong entourage, queuing to buy a Pritt Stick in a Poundland in Walsall.

Another favourite fact of Andy's is that Engels, after living in Hulme in the mid-1800s, swiftly went off to compose *The Condition of the Working Class in England* and then subsequently his half of *The Communist Manifesto*. That's got to be *even worse* than appearing in a *Crap Towns* volume.

TOASTER: JOE MARSHAL

FAVOURITE FACTS

- After working in his father's factory in Hulme, Friedrich Engels wrote *The Condition of the Working Class in England*, which led subsequently to him writing *The Communist Manifesto* with Karl Marx.

- It was portrayed in the Jeff Noon science fiction novel *Vurt* as 'Bottletown'.

- Hulme is home to the first Rolls-Royce factory, which opened in 1904.

- Every summer for ten years there was an annual 'Punk's Picnic' on the grassland in Hulme. Punks would come from all over Britain and Europe to help celebrate it.

- Home to The Dogs of Heaven, a performance company who performed huge and possibly not quite legal firework shows which contained abseiling, throwing cars off the tower blocks, burning Viking ships and illegal raves with dancing JCBs and dinosaurs!

> **SHAUN SEZ:** All very 'alternative', I'm sure, but could you please bear in mind some of us have jobs and children?

- Graffiti Jams were held every summer – with artists coming to use the flats that were about to be knocked down as their canvas – which appeared in several episodes of *Cracker*.

- The Hacienda was around 200 yards from Hulme – the venue that, aside from its other accomplishments, held the first ever UK wedding to be celebrated in a night club. Hulme was also home to hundreds of bands. At one time it seemed like every other flat was a rehearsal studio.

LOCAL HEROES

★ Jane Austen had a house on Boundary Lane.

> **SHAUN SEZ:** Luckily for her this was before Local Council Noise Abatement Orders were enforced, as Jane was a very noisy neighbour by all accounts, conducting 'wild and lecherous romps well into the night', punching neighbours in the face when they asked her to turn it down, and one complaining he saw her 'curling one off' in his driveway at 3 a.m.

★ Anthony Burgess went to school in Hulme.

★ Nico from Velvet Underground lived here in the seventies.

★ Kev Davey, the jazz trumpeter.

★ Home to Lou Rhodes and then later Andy Barlow from Lamb.

RIPON

Playlist

▷ **Nick Drake** – Northern Sky (as the skies here are truly massive. When driving the road into Ripon from the A1 it's not unusual to be able to spot a storm, a rainbow and blue skies in the same vista across the Dales)

▷ **KC And The Sunshine Band** – Sound That Funky Horn

FAVOURITE FACTS

- Ripon boasts the country's oldest grammar school, which William Hague left because he hated it. Richard Hammond did too. So it can't be that bad.

- The obelisk in the town square is the highest in the country and was said to have several gold sovereigns hidden at the top, until restoration work took place and no sovereigns were found.

- We have a ceremony that goes back over 1,100 years. It's the setting for the evening watch by the town hornblower. At 9 p.m. every night the hornblower, who dresses like Dick Turpin, comes out of the town hall and blows a buffalo horn four times to set the watch. He then jumps in his Ford Fiesta to drive off to find the Mayor and blows his horn wherever he may be and whatever he's doing (this is Ripon – it's never a 'she'). A few years ago the incumbent hornblower had to leave his post under a cloud after being stopped for drink-driving in possession of a large horn.

- Years ago, when horseback was the main method of transport, Ripon was the nation's centre for spur production.

- Ripon is the seventh-smallest city in the United Kingdom.

LOCAL HEROES

★ Patrick Stewart (Jean-Luc Picard from *Star Trek: TNG* amongst other things, of course) lived nearby for a long time, apparently, and was known to frequent W. H. Smith's in the square.

★ Wilfred Owen, the First World War poet, lived here while training for the trenches of France.

LEIGH

One's hometown always has a special gravitational pull. No matter how far one travels away from it, one can never escape its memories. I maintain a 'special relationship' with Leigh and frequently return to see friends and family. But perhaps the main reason I like to go back is that there are literally no decent chippies or pie shops in the Greater London area (discounting the posh ones that charge about nine quid for chips and fish, with no option of any 'pea wet' or fish crispy bits).

Leigh is an ex-cotton and mining town situated smack-bang (an antiquated geographical term) between Liverpool and Manchester on the A580. It resides in the borough of Wigan and is adjacent to Bolton, home of top Shaun Keaveny impersonator Peter Kay. It is home to a population of around 60,000 and has a pie shop for every eleven people in the population.

I have so very many memories of Leigh. Many of them fall within the three distinct boundaries of the Three 'B's . . .

1 BEER

Leigh, like many towns in this book, is awash with boozers in which the townsfolk temporarily obliterate the innate knowledge of their impending deaths with intoxicating liquor. The best way to communicate the wonders of Leigh pub culture is to describe the *Itinerary Do* to you. This was, in essence, a Leigh pub crawl devised by two friends of mine, John Ariss and Neil Unsworth, initially on the occasion of their joint birthdays. The Itinerary Do (present

****

tense as, remarkably, it's still going strong) is a pub crawl that takes in most notable Leigh pubs. The average time in each is around twenty minutes. Each participant is entered into a pre-drawn team, given a drinking 'handicap' and asked to participate in numerous imaginative/dangerous drinking games. Here is an example of some of the rules of engagement:

> 1 unit = 1 point
> Downed pint = double points
> Tactical chunder (or 'The Roman') = minus 5 points

Over the years this tournament has been host to all manner of casualties, yet, surprisingly, no fatalities. In many ways, there can be no winners in a game of such herculean irresponsibility, and, in effect, there aren't any, because every year without fail, everyone gets so smashed that no one can really remember who got the most points.

2 BAPS

Here are some of the great carbohydrate-vending emporiums of Leigh:

> **WATERFIELDS** (1988–present): the McDonald's of the north-west, this palace of pastry churns out so many pasties each week that, were they laid end to end, they would stretch all the way from Radcliffe's Bike Shop on Bradshawgate to H. Samuel jewellers' on Bradshawgate.

****

212   R2D2 LIVES IN PRESTON

CHARCOAL HOB (1985–91): purveyors of delicious barbecued meats of unknown provenance.

ROSE OF INDIA (1973–95): the scene of a hundred thousand orders of 'thhh hotttst curry you've got maaayte . . . NORRA VINDALOO! THEY'RE FOR PONCES!'

ROMINO'S (1986–99): creators of the ultimate 'hot and spicy' pizza. Grown men cried the day they boarded that place up. I know, 'cos I was him. The ground beef/flaked chilli/pepperoni mix was so pungent and bountifully administered, the day after consumption one would usually suffer the ill-effects in the form of a 'crescent moon'. This was a ferocious bowel ache that arced in a crescent shape in the bottom of your gut, until such time the offending matter could be expelled into a fortified toilet bowl.

GREENALGH'S (1957–present): Another great pie shop that delivered the 'slurpy' (a pie in a bap). Inexplicably, everyone still pronounces it 'GREEN HALCHES', even though this is clearly incorrect.

3 BANDS

Many of you will be waiting for the final treatise on the history of that greatest of unsigned bands, Mosque. Sadly, this is not it. Time and space will not permit that epic tale of ambition, excess, betrayal, lust and HobNobs to be told in its lurid entirety (for that we must wait for the unexpurgated biography currently being penned by Paul Morley). Instead, here is a brief history of the Leigh music scene of the late eighties:

MOSQUE: formed in August 1987 by John Ariss (singer), Paul Banks (bass), Martin Ormrod (guitar), Shaun Keaveny (guitar) and Damian Higgins (keyboard), the band, fuelled by a herculean work ethic, a shared love of early Yes and Dire Straits albums, HobNobs and oven chips, rapidly became known as one of the five best (or to put it more accurately, one of the five) bands on the (de)famed Leigh music circuit of 1988. Gripped with a creative fervour unseen since the early days of The Beatles or even Mud, the band soon amassed a canon of essential post-punk neo-classics like 'Bullet For Botha' (example lyric: 'I've got a bullet for Botha, hell lies waiting for you, you're just spitting on justice, with your fascist, boot, crew') and 'On The Level'. These already high-water marks were almost immediately superseded with more complex pieces such as 'Bloodspike' ('Bloodspike killed my best friend's cousin'), 'Ferry Strike' ('Paint my door, eat my lolly, focus my scripture, if you want') and 'RAF Biggin Hill' ('RAF Biggin Hill, RAF Benny Hill, RAF Friggin Hell'). Tragedy struck during this early apotheosis when founder member Orms announced during a steak bap at a practice in early 1988 that his parents, upon seeing his mock O Level results, had forbidden him to work with the band any more.

Despite losing a key member, the band soldiered on, and recruited fifteen-year-old manchild percussionist Leon Parr. Inspired by the new-found responsibility and rhythm section, sole guitarist Keaveny cranked up the guitar magic, which inspired lyricist Ariss to create some of his most profound and mystical statements. Highlights of this era of their development include 'M*A*S*H' (a song about the American TV show *M*A*S*H*), 'Lost Things' (a song about losing things) and their audacious, never-recorded concept album, *The Dr Nicholas Barden Mysteries*, a Bennet-esque odyssey into pharmacological mundanity, written in one afternoon whilst on the dole. There is much more to the rise and eventual Icarus-style fall of this greatest of bands, but for now the story must be laid to one side while we discuss other Leigh bands.

****

THOSE NAUGHTY CORINTHIANS (NÉS BARRY DIED OF IGNORANCE): another one of the great lost bands. Augmented in 1989 by on-loan Mosque bassist Banks. Best songs: 'GM Buses', 'Do The Ayatollah', 'Ermintrude', 'I Hate Cats'.

HYACINTH GARDEN: a goth band. The songs weren't that good, but Craig the guitarist always had good guitar pedals so he sounded a bit like Billy Duffy. Which is always nice.

NEIL GYRATES ON TUESDAYS: contenders for the Half Man Half Biscuit comedy rock title. No song titles remain in the memory, but I think they had a song about Cliff Richard losing his virginity.

So there it is. Leigh. A town of mystery, complexity, beer and pasties. Much like the Mississippi Delta, it was a verdant musical pasture. Perhaps it's the proximity to the water (Leigh Canal), perhaps it's what they put in that water (dead dogs in carrier bags). Whatever it is, it makes Leigh a place of unique artistic heritage.

YORK

TOASTER: CHARLOTTE MCGRATH

Playlist

▷ **Franz Ferdinand** – Take Me Out (Martyn Clayton
is a writer who lives just opposite me and has written
a book called *Take Me Out*)

▷ **Shed 7** – Going For Gold

▷ **One Night Only** – Just For Tonight

FAVOURITE FACTS

➤ York has been protected by encompassing walls ever
since Roman times. These are called the City Walls, Bar
Walls or Roman Walls (although very little of the Roman
stonework is still there, and the walls take a different
course than they did in those times). You can legally
shoot a Scotsman with a bow and arrow from the Bar
Walls (except on Sundays).

➤ York Minster is the largest Gothic cathedral north
of the Alps and contains half of the medieval stained
glass in Britain.

➤ York is home of Rowntree's (now Nestlé) and Terry's
Chocolate. So we gave birth to Fruit Pastilles, Fruit
Gums and Chocolate Orange!

****

- There are 365 pubs within the Bar Walls, one for every day of the year.

- The famous York races sprang up only as a sideshow to add to the entertainment of the hangings!

LOCAL HEROES

★ Guy Fawkes

★ Frankie Howerd

★ Judi Dench

★ Marco Gabbiadini

★ Steve McClaren

★ Shed Seven come from York, and were named after the bit of the factory they used to work in.

★ Chris Helme, singer for The Seahorses, and a friend of mine!

★ John Barry, composer who wrote the James Bond theme tune.

★ 'Hunter' from the *Gladiators* TV show actually lived in my street – I saw him often. He went out with Ulrika while living here, although I only saw her once in a car.

★ I once met Mick Hucknall (Simply Red) in the York Arms pub in the late eighties (he was seeing a girl who lived here).

★ Ian Kelsey, actor in *Casualty* and *Emmerdale*.

WAKEFIELD

In the interests of transparency it is perhaps worth mentioning that everything you read in this 'book' is not *necessarily* stone-cold proven-beyond-doubt empirical provable positivist fact. I realize this may come as a salutary shock to those History A-Level teachers that were about to order a thousand copies for their school, but there it is. Toaster Alan says in his toast of wonderful Wakefield, that: '"Here We Go Round The Mulberry Bush" originates from Wakefield prison. It used to be a mixed prison with a mulberry bush in the middle – visiting children used to play around the bush and sing this song.' I have to contest that this was ever the case. I mean, I *know* we've become a lot more child-oriented and fear-dominated as the centuries have trundled by, but are we *really* to believe that, even in the Middle Ages, any self-respecting parent would let their kids go and play in the local PRISON? I had trouble persuading me mam to let me play in the cul-de-sac for fear of abduction or traffic tragedy, never mind swinging my Grifter round to bloody STRANGEWAYS for an afternoon with Fingers, Stabby and Little Bob Hoskins from F-Wing! Imagine that parental permission request?

(Lute music in the background. Perhaps a sound effect of a man having his gammy leg sawn off as ambient background noise.)
MEDIEVAL CHILD: Verily, Mama, can I pop over to the local prison to make merry with the thieves, sodomites and killers? They have a wonderful mulberry bush, Consumptive

Willie, and I like to dance round!
MEDIEVAL MOTHER: Yes.

Not bloody likely.

On a personal note, I sank many a good pint in Wakefield's plethora of pubs back in the nineties. My friends Ste and Dom were student actors at the local Bretton Hall college. Though their dreams of Hollywood superstardom never quite came to fruition, they did enjoy more sex and drugs than I did, and Ste played an evil character in *EastEnders* who battered Phil Mitchell half to death in a back alley. I couldn't have been more proud of my own son.

TOASTER: ALAN BENNETT

Playlist

▷ **The Killers** – All The Things That I've Done

FAVOURITE FACTS

- The mnemonic 'Richard Of York Gave Battle In Vain' (traditionally used to help small children recall the order of the colours of the rainbow) refers to the Battle of Wakefield, which took place during the War of the Roses. 'The Grand Old Duke Of York' is based on the same battle!

- Another nursery rhyme, 'Here We Go Round The Mulberry Bush', originates from Wakefield prison.

****

It used to be a mixed prison with a mulberry bush in the middle – visiting children used to play around the bush and sing this song.

- All the exterior shots in *A Touch of Frost* were filmed in Wakefield.

- The first ever zoo anywhere in the world was opened in Wakefield in the nineteenth century.

LOCAL HEROES

★ Robin Hood was reputed to be from Wakefield (not Nottingham).

★ The Cribs

★ Black Lace

BARNSLEY

TOASTER: MATTHEW KEEN

FAVOURITE FACTS

- During the miners' strikes my dad saw an advert for a second-hand fridge in the paper and went round to have a look. When it opened, who slowly put his head round the door but a very cautious Arthur Scargill, who was then asked if he was selling a fridge. I think you can imagine the reaction.

- My mum used to live near one of the members of Saxon, but she can't remember which one, only that he had a mullet.

LOCAL HEROES

★ Brian Glover

★ Saxon was formed in, and has several members from, Barnsley.

★ Michael Parkinson

HARROGATE

**'HARROGATE DISTRICT IS AN
EXPERIENCE FOR EVERYONE'**
Harrogate Council Website

I think it was Oscar Wilde who said 'brevity is the soul of wit'. The reason I think this is a) because I haven't read enough books, so therefore attribute all pithy witticisms to either him or Shakespeare, and b) 'cos he was a proper smartarse. Anyway, whoever it was wot said it had a good point. Examples of brevity of wit are legion, but it has in my mind never been better illustrated than by a group of local children who, upon seeing my friends on their way to a fancy-dress party made up to look like the musketeers, shouted, 'Ey look! It's the Musker-Queers!'

Granted this is both non-PC and mildly offensive, but as an improvised quickfire gag it betters anything you'll see on Friday-night TV.

Toaster Alison below employs the brevity/wit principle well here with her short-but-sweet toast of Harrogate. Yes, there is much to recommend this gorgeous and historical town but, as Alison instinctively knows, most historical facts are quite dry for a brekkie show, so she's boiled it down to the TTN mainstays of a comedy museum, an unsubstantiated fact involving an iconic historical figure and one of many mentions of the world-famous Betty's Tea Rooms.

TOASTER: ALISON THOMAS

FAVOURITE FACTS

- Harrogate is home to Betty's famous tea shops, owned by Taylors of Harrogate and the company who make Yorkshire Tea. Continuing the theme, it's also famous for spas and water-cures, dating back to 1571.

- The National Rhubarb collection is to be found here.

- When Agatha Christie disappeared in 1926 she was found in a Harrogate hotel, claiming to be suffering from amnesia.

- Charles Dickens once said that Harrogate is full of crazy people.

- Harrogate also has a particularly awesome conference centre.

> **SHAUN SEZ:** By all accounts, Harrogate's Conference Centre is second to NONE. I don't get invited to many conferences, but I am holding out hope that the next one that comes along will be in the hallowed halls of the HCC, as I prefer to call it. I hear they have pull-down screens and 1080 hi-def projectors IN EVERY ROOM!

LOCAL HEROES

- ★ Andy Gray (footballer, but not the famous one).

- ★ No one else

****

CLITHEROE

As we can see here by Toaster Mark's entry, there is much to recommend Clitheroe to the general populace. It is the dead centre of Britain. It has a claim to a revolutionary scientific innovation (the jet engine). It contains a very small castle. It was even name-checked on the internationally-renowned-yet-utterly-baffling-and-incredulous American TV series *Lost* (the only TV show whose title has become a self-fulfilling prophecy for its writers). But one of *my* favourite facts about Clitheroe is that, alongside Scunthorpe, it is the only northern town I can think of that contains within it a rude sexual term. In fact, if one removes the 'e' from the end and provides a space, one transforms the otherwise dull place name into CLIT HERO! I have taken the trouble to write a short story about this new superhero:

IN DOWNTOWN NEW YORK, A SINGLE WOMAN IS BATTLING WITH URGES SHE CANNOT CONTROL . . . UNABLE TO GLEAN SATISFACTION FROM HOUSEHOLD APPLIANCES OR YOUTUBE RERUNS OF MICHAEL BUBLÉ CONCERTS, SHE TURNS TO THE ONLY MAN WHO CAN SAVE HER FROM SEXUAL FRUSTRATION . . . HIS NAME? CLIT HERO!

I'll leave it there.

TOASTER: MARK

Playlist

▷ **Lieutenant Pigeon** – Mouldy Old Dough

FAVOURITE FACTS

☞ The jet engine was invented in Clitheroe,
by Sir Frank Whittle.

☞ Clitheroe is the most central town in Britain.

☞ It has the smallest castle (technically a 'keep')
in the UK, but officially the largest pigeons!

☞ Incredibly, it was name-checked in *Lost* – Charlie refers
to it as 'the arse-end of nowhere'.

LOCAL HEROES

★ Sir Frank Whittle

★ Thelma Barlow (better known as Mavis from *Corrie*)
has been known to shop there!

SHAUN SEZ: Thelma aka Mavis has been much
missed by Corrie fans since she left the
show, but none so much as 'comedian',
'actor' and 'entertainer' Bobby Davro, who
had, up to that point, built an entire
career on his impression of the character.
All together now: 'MMMMM, RITA . . . WELL I
DONN'T REEEEEALLY KNOOOOOW . . .

****

SCARBOROUGH

Some areas of the country, such as Rusholme (Ruffians), (The Only Living Boy In) New Cross and Scarborough (Fair) have a bespoke song all ready and waiting for a Nation Toaster to request. But that was a path of too-little resistance for our Scarborough Toaster, who instead chose the Stones anthem of outdoor altercation as his number. This due to the fact that, as well as being one of the UK's premier seaside towns of the sixties and seventies, Scarborough has a history of bloody battles that belie its chintzy fish 'n' chips image. Perhaps because of its coastal aspect, and being so close to the European low countries, it's been battered more times than Heston Blumenthal's saveloy.

A surely more shocking fact is that celebrated newsreader and sock-wearer Jon Snow, during a student protest in the sixties, hurled a tin of paint, Stone Roses-style, at the local statue of our great widow, Queen Victoria! Jon, how *could* you? Conjure *that* image the next time you see him grilling the Liberian Ambassador to London about unpaid congestion charge fines! This fact did give me pause for poignant reflection. How sad that a man as fiery and free-spirited as Jon has been neutered of his naughtiness by his lofty position. How great would it be to see Jon Snow present the Channel 4 Evening News 'live from a holding cell in Blackfriars' after knocking a policeman's helmet off with a snowball filled with dogshit? Well, a guy can dream...

TOASTER: TOM OULTON

Playlist

▷ **Primal Scream** – Rocks

▷ **Street Fighting Man** – The Rolling Stones

▷ **Anarchy In The UK** – The Sex Pistols
(in recognition of Jon Snow's sterling work!)

FAVOURITE FACTS

➤ The bloke who is known as the Father of English Geology,
William 'Strata' Smith, was based in Scarborough! Like
all good nineteenth-century scientists he was a complete
amateur, but made a map of the geological rocks of Britain
that remains essentially unchanged today.

➤ The Holbeck Hall Hotel, which once stood on the
cliff tops, infamously slipped away into the sea back
in '92/'93.

➤ In the Second World War Scarborough was the first place
in Britain to take civilian casualties after a German naval
ship shelled the old town. About eighty people were killed.

➤ Jon Snow (Channel 4 news reader) attended Yorkshire
Coast College in Scarborough. Allegedly he was
involved in a protest in which he threw a tin of paint
at Scarborough's statue of Queen Victoria.

➤ It's always been quite a violent place – it was fought over
by Romans, Vikings, Cavaliers and Roundheads, mods

and rockers in the sixties, and more recently outside the club XS pretty much every night.

- The first ever armoured vehicle was assembled at Burniston Barracks in Scarborough.

LOCAL HEROES

★ Robert Palmer's from Scarborough. So too were the Little Angels (early nineties soft-rock combo).

★ Elizabeth Dawn, who plays Vera Duckworth on *Corrie*.

★ Sir Jimmy Savile has a home there and is often to be seen around the place. Sir Jimmy even has a bench with a plaque on it that reads 'Jimmy Savile – But not just yet'.

WARRINGTON

Like many a hormone-harried hair-sprouting teen, I fell in love a lot as a kid. A LOT. I think my first love affair was with Cheryl Spencer in Junior One (do they call that Year 3 now?), but that was doomed to failure, as she only had eyes for Paul Roach. Like many of my subsequent paramours, she never even knew I liked her. This pattern of love-via-stealth, or affection avoidance, repeated itself like a cucumber, through Alex Gildart and Jackie Mason (not the elderly Jewish comedian) all the way up to perhaps my most ardent and long-lasting pointless, unrequited love affair, with the goddess of womankind herself, Juliet Wood. (Well, Juliet Woodn't, as it turns out. Not with me at any rate.)

This failure-strewn highway of disappointment leads us up to Sixth Form, and the early nineties. By this point, my friends and I (because they were equally rubbish with women) were seething, broiling, cauldrons of untapped desire. We were finding it at least as hard to be noticed by women as Pete Docherty seems to be by non-lenient magistrates. In short, we weren't getting ANY. Single-cell amoebas were getting more sex than us. (That's the kind of joke we might have made at the time also, as many of us were taking Biology A-level, with the alluring yet achingly unattainable Miss Hayes. As her eyelashes fluttered, so did our hearts.) We would release the resulting pressure in relatively safe, non-sexual ways, by playing ludicrously dangerous games like Death Football (like football but crossed with violent assault), The Board of Death (a game in which one protagonist would be trapped against a wall while the others would violently wobble a large piece of board on to his head until mercy was begged. I know what you're thinking: How could these guys *not* have got laid?), and one of my favourites, by engaging in jazz dancing at Mister Smith's nightclub, Warrington, mentioned here by Toaster Kath Brown.

During all of this time, one woman we could all rely on was Michaela Strachan. She presented *The Hitman and Her* with Pete Waterman, and the show would often be filmed at Mister Smith's. For every young man with a dangerous and undirected amount of testosterone, Michaela was an archangel of lust. We would fall into our houses after a night on the town having been mercilessly and relentlessly ignored by every XX-chromosomed being within a 20-mile radius only to click on the telly and see magisterial Michaela, gyrating innocently in hotpants that defied the broadcasting edicts of the times. For that reason, Ms Strachan will always be one of my Wonders of the Solar System. Thank you to Toaster Kath for resurrecting those deep-seated memories. Now I can finally move on.

TOASTER: KATH BROWN

Playlist

▷ **Stone Roses** – Mersey Paradise

FAVOURITE FACTS

➤ *The Hitman and Her* (the late eighties/early nineties music show starring Michaela Strachan and Pete Waterman) used to be broadcast from the town's premier night spot, Mister Smith's.

****

- Oliver Cromwell crossed the river at the now famous Bridge Foot nearby and is reputed to have stayed in a house in the town centre.

LOCAL HEROES

★ There are numerous minor celebrities connected to the town, including J from 5ive, Kerry Katona and Comedy Dave.

> **SHAUN SEZ:** My cousin's hubby Shaun is the cousin of J from 5ive. FACT. Many people mistake me for Gary Barlow's fatter, uglier, hairier, less musically talented, less successful, less sexually alluring sibling. They are wrong.

★ Ian Brown was born in Warrington and still has a house in the environs.

ST HELENS

TOASTER: KERRY ALDERSON

> **Playlist**
>
> ▷ **Blondie** – Heart Of Glass (Pilkington's Glass was traditionally the town's biggest employer)

FAVOURITE FACTS

- Johnny Vegas had longest acceptance speech ever for a British Comedy award in 2001. During the speech he thanked 'everyone who drinks in the Springfield' – my local!

- We have a regular feature in our local paper, the *Reporter*, where they name and shame everyone who has appeared in court that week with full name address and all details of the court appearance. For instance it might be something like: 'John Smith pleaded guilty to stealing a packet of bacon from Asda' (that's quite a common one). Everyone loves to read it to see if they recognize any names!

LOCAL HEROES

★ Warrior from TV's *Gladiators* hails from here.

CARLISLE

It's funny what kids lie about, isn't it? I remember when I started secondary school, pretending that my dad had a Honda Prelude. Not exactly Walter Mitty that, is it? Much more impressive was a friend of ours, Andy who claimed to have invented a machine that could teleport humans down phone lines. The only drawback to his invention, apparently, was that, despite the fact it could transmit and reassemble complex DNA structures and the like, it couldn't do the same for trainers, so people would arrive at the other end shoeless. Another fantasist at school called Carl had me believe there was an island just off the coast of Scotland called Carlisle, and that it was in fact named after him by his father, a wealthy landowner. Quite why a man so prosperous who could afford to buy an island could only stretch himself to rent a tenement terrace for his family in Higher Folds was a question that didn't occur to me at the time.

I must confess that I have never visited Carlisle, that most northerly of English cities. I feel like a fool. After all, if it's good enough for former US President Woodrow Wilson it's good enough for me. It's a high coup for any toasted town to be able to claim a US president as a visitor, presiding, retired or dead.

That said, Wigan couldn't move for the bastards the year I did my Job Club there. In the midst of his tumultuous period of office, Bill Clinton flew out to the town to open a branch of Clinton's Cards, and I once had to queue behind former president and peanut magnate Jimmy Carter for a meat and potato at Poole's Pie Shop while he showed off his Nobel Peace Prize. I think his brother-in-law lived in Worsley...

TOASTER: RICHARD WEIR

Playlist

▷ **The Smiths** – Panic (for the immortal line 'But there's Panic on the streets of Carlisle', which brought an almighty cheer when they played here on the opening night of 'The Queen Is Dead' tour, 13 October '86. I still have the crumpled and ragged ticket somewhere – not bad for a first ever gig)

FAVOURITE FACTS

- Her Majesty's theatre in Carlisle was the first to be lit by electricity, in 1880.

- Carlisle was the main centre for 'The State Management Scheme', where the Government took over and ran the brewing, distribution and sale of liquor, from 1916 to 1973. The scheme was an attempt to reduce drunkenness and its effects on the huge number of workers from the nearby munitions factory supplying armaments in the First World War. So we had binge drinking ninety years ago, it ain't a new thing ... Can you believe, the scheme had a 'No treating' policy, from 1916 to 1919, whereby rounds could not be bought!

- The mother of the US President Woodrow Wilson was born in Carlisle, and he visited the city in 1896, returning

****

to the Lake District a further four times in the next twelve years, he liked it so much. To mark this historical connection, J D Wetherspoon named their first Carlisle pub after him.

- The first pillarbox went up on Botchergate, in Carlisle, in 1853.

LOCAL HEROES

★ The drummer in punk band The Germs loved the city so much she changed her name to ... Belinda Carlisle – and gave up drumming in dodgy punk bands.

> **SHAUN SEZ:** I sat next to 'The Voice', Elaine Paige, at the Ivor Novello Awards once and she told me her great-great-granddad was responsible for building Blackpool Tower. Who knew?

SHEFFIELD

Playlist

▷ **Roisin Murphy** – Overpowered

FAVOURITE FACTS

- Sheffield is England's greenest city, with over 150 woodlands, and approximately fifty public parks.

- Mary Queen of Scots was held under house arrest in Sheffield for fourteen years.

- The inventor of Sheffield plate, Thomas Boulsover, came from Sheffield, as did the inventor of stainless steel, Harry Brearley.

LOCAL HEROES

★ Sean Bean

★ Sheffield has a rich musical heritage, including (but not limited to): Heaven 17, Human League, Arctic Monkeys, Pulp, Richard Hawley, Def Leppard, Bruce Dickinson, Graham Fellows (John Shuttleworth), Martin Fry (ABC), Babybird and Moloko (hence the Roisin Murphy link).

****

BRADFORD

Curry. I'll say it again, curry. If I type the word one more time, just like that terrifying titular Candyman in the horror film of the same name, the words will become embodied in reality, and you, the reader, will be POWERLESS to resist ordering a massive takeaway tikka and naan upon your return home. SUCH IS THE POWER OF CURRY!

Good friends of mine will know that I have an obsession with curry that borders on the maniacal. Once, nine years ago, some friends and I decided we would hire a little caravan in a sleepy corner of Pembrokeshire in order to enjoy a nice relaxing getaway. (What in reality happened was we each bought a BB pistol in the town of Tenby and spent five solid days holed up inside said caravan enacting some kind of proto-*World of Warcraft* scene within. The horror...)

One night, after a particularly gruelling afternoon gun battle (Atherton Boys beat the Leithers one partial-blinding to nil), we decided to repair to the town centre for a few restorative pints and, we hoped, a curry. We arrived at the town and began to slowly panic as no Indian restaurant could be seen. Suddenly I was gripped by a primal and hitherto unrecognized instinct. I thrust my nose into the air, Scooby-style, grabbed my mate Chris by the arm and whispered with import, 'Follow me.' Like a man on a mission, or a drug hound sensing a kilo of smack up someone's crackpipe, I strode purposefully through the

Tenby thoroughfares until I found what I was sure I had smelled some 500 metres away: in all its garlic-infused glory, THE BAY OF BENGAL!

So, yes, as I said, I like curry. As do the people of Bradford. It is something for which they are rightly famous. Thankfully, Toasters Damian and Laura bring us more than just curry, including a nice hangman fact. I wonder how many people have curry as a last meal? I know I would...

TOASTERS: DAMIEN BOVÉ
LAURA

Playlist

▷ **Hot Hot Heat** – This Town

▷ **Terrorvision** – Alice What's The Matter

FAVOURITE FACTS

- In 2006 Bradford was named UK's fattest city. This could be due to having nearly 400 curry houses in the district.

- On 28 October 1907 Bradford was the first local authority in Britain to introduce school meals. The first meal was porridge and stewed fruit.

****

- The place is so action-packed that my local village (Cullingworth) was thrown into uproar recently over plans to move a bus stop 100 yards up the street.

- In 2007 Bradford hosted first UK Bombay-mix-eating competition. The winners ate over 2lb of Bombay mix in sixty seconds!

SHAUN SEZ: Of course, any man, after seven or eight pints of export-strength lager, made to wait in an Indian restaurant foyer, will be easily able to put away at least double that amount in half the time. I reckon my mate Banksy (one of the great curry chefs of my acquaintance) could put away a good kilo in half a minute.

- Bradford used to be the wool capital of the world. However, it's now billed as the curry capital of the world.

- I (Damien) am a former student of the district and as such I can truthfully report Bradford is home of the £1 pint and, on one infamous occasion, was home to the *10p a pint night* – it was a great city to get educated in.

- It's a popular urban myth about Bradford that it has more curry houses than Calcutta (Kolkata), but, actually, this can't be true.

- It has a strong political history: the Labour Party was founded in the city in 1893.

****

- The city was also home to Britain's last hangman, Albert Pierrepoint.

LOCAL HEROES

★ Bradford has a strong tradition of producing major figures in the world of the arts, and some of the greatest artistic figures of the twentieth century hail from there: Fredrick Delius, David Hockney, J. B. Priestley and Richard Whiteley, although some people claim that Whiteley was not a great artist.

Other famous people from the area include:

★ Gareth Gates

★ Kimberly from Girls Aloud.

****

★ Terrorvision, a band that, while officially being from Keighley (just down the road), are always quoted as being a Bradford band and were often seen gigging in the pubs around the city in the early days.

★ Cullingworth was once home to Olympic swimmer Duncan Goodhew.

MONTON

Young love. It burns like a harrowing sun in the chest, immolating all other thoughts and engulfing the heart like a forest fire. The object of desire, so impossibly beautiful, so untouchably erotic, so as to render the stricken completely inert, collapsed and engorged in contortions of lust and grief at the thought of not being with the desired for even a moment.

It was a bit like that for me in 1989 when I, in my pomegranate-faced pimply pomp, fell in love with the lovely and loveable Jackie. Oh, how my heart LEAPED to see her Adidas cagoule on the hanger in the common room! I sighed with uncontainable pleasure whenever she flirtatiously engaged me in chat! "Av yer got a pen?' she would ask, when I knew what she was *really* asking was, 'Will you be mine forever?' And how my loins would CREAK when she ate a creme egg!

Eventually my ardour was fanned as she became interested in me. No doubt beguiled by my sizzling wit, my resemblance to a younger, more emaciated, spottier Ben Volpierre-Pierrot (from Curiosity Killed The Cat), my bleach-wash jeans and encyclopaedic knowledge of The Wedding Present! Sadly, like Romeo and Juliet, our love was thwarted. She was betrothed to another, thick-set Kevin Cuddy, and my heart was broken. He promised that my face was too. Luckily this never came to fruition. I had to wait eighteen more months to lose my virginity, but we won't let that detain us here.

Anyway, Jackie came from Monton. Though it's just a northern town, to me, the word was impossibly romantic

****

and beautiful then. Monton . . . (Try it like Gainsbourg would say it: *Mon-tonn!*) Not only is it responsible for Jackie, Queen bloody Victoria went through it on a barge once too! In many ways, I, like Vic, have been wearing black and mourning the love of *my* life since that heady winter of '89. She had her Albert, I had my Jackie. (Fade out to *Love Story* theme.)

(N.B. If my wife Lucy is reading this, I am, *of course*, exaggerating for comic effect, and I virtually never think of Jackie any more. Certainly not since the extensive electro-shock treatments I endured in California in the late nineties. BIG KISS!)

TOASTER: ELLIE POTTS

Playlist

▷ **Arcade Fire** – The Well And The Lighthouse

FAVOURITE FACTS

- Queen Victoria passed through Monton on her royal barge in 1851; she stopped but didn't get off! Just near where she stopped, a guy called Phil Austin has built a lighthouse next to the canal, to commemorate the moment.

- We also have Eccles nearby, and obviously I have to give a shout-out for the humble Eccles cake (also known as 'dead fly pie'), which is famous all over the world.

****

LOCAL HEROES

★ We have a couple of TV celebrities currently living in
Monton. One is Dev from *Corrie*, the other is Christopher
Eccleston, ex-Doctor Who!

SALE

I am particularly enamoured of the musical points made in this toast by James. First off, one can't pass by the following sentence without comment: 'The Waterside Centre has recently hosted gigs from Midge Ure and The Zombies'. Though I am almost certain that is supposed to denote two separate music acts, I couldn't help wondering if Midge Ure and the zombies was just a perfect description of any of Midge's audiences these days. (I must at this point immediately retract that cruel and poor joke and stress what a lovely, self-effacing and charming man Midge is. He came on the show once! And he wrote 'Vienna'!)

The other musical fact I want to mention (apart from the fact that BBC 6 Music and Fall legend Marc Riley is or was a resident) is the one about David Gray living in Sale. Where I come from, this doyen of dour, this sultan of self-reflection, this master of the mawkish is known not as David Gray, but instead, as Owd Wobble Yead. This because you will notice, when he performs, he has an uncontrollable urge to wobble his head from side to side *so viciously* that he has to have a top osteopath travel everywhere with him on the road. The wobble is so extreme that physicists from the Department of Perpetual Motion and Renewable Energy Research Institute, based at UCLA, California, have studied it and drawn up plans to have David Gray power a small town in Norway whenever he tours. David Gray was also responsible for a song that best describes my radio style: 'Babylon'.

****

TOASTER: JAMES

> **Playlist**
>
> ▷ **David Gray** – Please Forgive Me
>
> ▷ **Cake** – The Distance

FAVOURITE FACTS

► Sale is home to Sale Water Park, an artificial lake which was created when the land was excavated to make the M60 motorway. The Waterside Centre next door has recently hosted gigs from Midge Ure and The Zombies.

► During the Battle of Britain, Sale was attacked in what's known as the Manchester Blitz. On 23 December 1940 over 600 incendiary bombs were dropped on Sale in three hours, and incredibly no one was hurt, but the town hall was severely damaged.

LOCAL HEROES

★ During his Radio 1 days Marc Riley lived here. (He might do still – I think I saw him the other day driving a Mercedes estate.)

> **SHAUN SEZ:** Marc Riley – one of the understated greats of radio, and a top man to go for a pint with.

****

★ David Gray lived in the town during his younger years.

★ Robert Bolt, who wrote the screenplays for *Lawrence of Arabia*, *Dr Zhivago* and *A Man for All Seasons*, lived in the town and has a theatre named after him.

★ Ian Brown lived near the Brooklands area of the town.

> **SHAUN SEZ:** Ian Brown — a man who I have never been for a pint with, but I would like to. Mind you, I'm not convinced Browny would be up for a pint these days. If it closes the deal, Ian, I am happy to go for a chai latte or even a green tea.

★ Everton defender Phil Jagielka was born and lived in the town. Lou Macari, of Manchester United and chip shop fame, also lived in Sale.

SUNDERLAND

If by nothing else, I am impressed with the sheer front and hubris of our Sunderland Toaster, Julia, who claims in bold black and white here that her hometown of Sunderland 'invented glass'! Sunderland invented glass, did it? I suppose Ross Millard from The Futureheads invented the internet as well, did he? And Lauren Laverne was the first person to map the human genome? Even I know that glass was invented by the Sumerians in 3000 BC! And I didn't even have to quickly check Wikipedia to find that out! (Closes laptop shiftily.)

That oversight aside, we thank Julia for her contribution, though it includes the grisly claim to fame that Sid James died onstage in Sunderland. Wouldn't it be wonderful to think that the last sound you'd hear as you slipped from this world into the great unknown would be the sound of a crowd's laughter? Unless, like a friend of my uncle's, the crowd are laughing because you've collapsed with a heart attack in a nightclub while dressed as Mister Blobby.

Finally, this Toast begs the question: is it better to be known as 'Britain's Biggest Town', or to be upgraded to city status, only to find you're merely Mister Medium? I always think it's best to be a big fish in a small pond. That's why I was proud to be Britain's Oldest Sixth Former for the fifth time as a twenty-three-year-old in 1994.

****

TOASTER: JULIA EMMERSON

Playlist

▷ **Kenickie** – Come Out 2nite

FAVOURITE FACTS

- Sid James died on stage at the Sunderland Empire.

- Glass was invented here.

- Sunderland used to be Europe's largest town until 1992, when it was turned into a city.

LOCAL HEROES

★ Kate Adie

★ Kenickie and The Futureheads are from Sunderland.

> **SHAUN SEZ:** It's wonderful to count both these musical Mackem heroes as friends and acquaintances of mine. Indeed, true Futurehead/Keaveny devotees will already know they can see my acting debut in the 2008 video that accompanies the 'Heads' song 'Walking Backwards', in which I get into a fist fight with a bunch of lairy puppets. Now I know how Russell Harty felt when he faced down the wrath of Emu.

****

★ L. S. Lowry painted here.

★ Lewis Carroll used to come and stay nearby – he wrote 'Jabberwocky' while staying in Whitburn – and he was apparently inspired by the place to create a lot of the contents of Wonderland.

HULL

Hull is one of Yorkshire's biggest cities, and resides on the east coast, on the Humber river, served since the seventies by the imposing and elegant Humber Bridge. It's known by many as something of an eyesore, a flat, grey, drizzle-drenched antithesis to the post-bomb brilliance of Manchester. But such a clichéd description does not do justice to a place so vibrant with ideas, people and culture.

I know 'cos my mate Banksy lived there. No, not that one, *he* wreaks arty havoc in the Brizzle area. No, this Banksy was my erstwhile Mosque bandmate Paul Banks: librarian, libertarian, curry chef, bassist and art terrorist of the first order.

Paul first decamped to Yorkshire's San Francisco in 1991 and quickly made numerous connections with a host of like-minded noiseniks, free thinkers and Aldi-frequenters. Before long he'd set up his first band, Popchrist (slogan, JESUS SAVES! POPCHRIST SCORES ON THE REBOUND!), and by 1994 he asked me to drum at a gig they'd booked at the local music mecca, The Adelphi. As this trip would provide ample opportunity to combine my favourite pastimes (drinking, socializing, showing off and making noise), I immediately agreed.

The journey to Hull on the East Coast Mainline from Leeds is much like life itself. It starts with hilly promise and romantic sweeps, gets a bit boring in the middle, and pretty ugly and messy at the end. Despite its dour countenance, though, it holds much promise for young students hoping to get smashed. With great alacrity Paul and his band of Popchristians showed me many of the sights that Hull had to offer, such as pubs like the Wellington, but by far the most memorable was Spiders. It is set out of town in an unprepossessing industrial estate, and once inside you are transported to another world. A dingy (not to be confused with dinghy), dank, mysterious place with wrought iron spiders' webs separating the many cavernous covens, it plays incredible music (upon my first visit I was greeted by the strains of Zep's 'Babe I'm Gonna Leave You') and serves leg-numbing pint-glass 'cocktails', the like of which you will never experience anywhere else ever. On my first visit, I had numerous Cuban Black Widows (a quid for a triple white rum, lime juice, coke, served with a jelly spider), inexplicably developed a Scouse accent, attempted to pass myself off as ex-Labour council leader Derek Hatton, passed out and came to four hours later emptying myself into a stranger's toilet. They say youth is wasted on the young. As far as I can see, youth is just wasted. (Please drink responsibly. Especially triple white rum cocktails.)

Sorry, where was I? Vomiting . . . Derek Hatton . . . Spiders . . . I remember, Popchrist! Yes! The next day, despite the physical handicap of being massively collectively hungover, the band managed to put on a barnstorming performance at The Adelphi (one of the best music venues in the country). Songs like 'Manic Street Nietzsche' and 'Where's Me Chips' (a meditation on feminism and chippy orders, sample lyric: 'WHERE'S ME F****N' CHIPS? *DO YOU WANT A PICKLED EGG?'*) received rapturous receptions, and we, the band members, were carried shoulder-high through the streets of Hull in triumph! (OK, this isn't true. I *was* carried out, but not of The Adelphi, rather out of Spiders, on my second visit in two days, this time covered in a film of unidentified sick.)

****

Popchrist was not the only noiseart/earache rock collective Banks managed to form. There was the terse angry sex of Tartrazine, and perhaps Banks's best-known Hull-based project, Santa's Buggerboyz. Described on their MySpace page as De Do Do Do, De Da Da Dadaists and comprised mainly of Banksy and his mate Bruce, a theremin player, occasionally my brother Paul on drums and the Heisenberg Uncertainty principle, the Buggerboyz are to musical harmony what Nick Griffin is to racial harmony. In 1999 they created an album a week for the whole year. Though much of the output was as easy-listening as a shed of cats on fire, there were numerous glimpses of satirical genius, with titles as adventurous and evocative as *Hi Honey I'm Homo!* (a concept album about a man coming out to his wife), *20 Nazi Golden Greats*, and the emotive Radiohead homage, *1K Computer* (complete with a ZX81 on the cover)

So there it is, my little love letter to the city of Hull. Thank you for the music!

TOASTER: MAC

Playlist

▷ **Salako** – Hull's Too Good For England

▷ **The Housemartins** – Sitting On A Fence

FAVOURITE FACTS

- Hull is the home of 'Chip Spice', a seasoning for chips which you cannot find anywhere else! It's sometimes known as 'American Chip Spice', even though it's got nothing to do with the US, and Americans don't even call them chips anyway.

- Hull's proper name is Kingston-Upon-Hull. It is home to the Humber Bridge, which is the third-longest single-span suspension bridge, and to the smallest window in the world (to be found at the George Hotel).

- Not only these, it also has the strangest street name as well: The Land of Green Ginger. No one knows the explanation for this name.

LOCAL HEROES

★ Maureen Lipman

★ William Wilberforce

★ Amy Johnson (the first female pilot).

★ John Cambridge (sometime Bolan drummer).

★ Roy North (presented *The Basil Brush Show*).

★ Roland Gift (Fine Young Cannibals).

Local bands:

★ The Housemartins

★ Beautiful South

★ The Paddingtons

★ Salako

DONCASTER

**'VISITORS TO DONCASTER WILL BE
PLEASANTLY SURPRISED'**
Official website

TOASTER: MATT HINDLE

> **Playlist**
>
> ▷ **The View** – The Don (in honour of the River Don)

FAVOURITE FACTS

- Thomas Crapper (inventor of the toilet) was born in Doncaster – St Lawrence's church (in Hatfield village) has had a stained glass window installed that depicts a toilet, to commemorate Crapper's work.

****

- Doncaster Mansion House is one of only four surviving civic mansion houses (the official residence of a town's mayor) in England. The others are in London, Bristol and York.

- The Mallard and the Flying Scotsman, two of the most famous trains in the history of the railways, were both built in Doncaster.

- Doncaster Dome boasts the largest fitness facility in the North of England. It's called The Fitness Village.

LOCAL HEROES

★ Johnny Shentall is one of Doncaster's most impressive exports. Originally in pop group Boom!, he went on to replace Kym Marsh when she left Hear'Say and is now married to Lisa Scott-Lee (he featured heavily in *Totally Scott-Lee* on MTV). I don't know why I brought it up, actually, because I've got no interest in him at all.

★ Leslie Garrett

★ Kevin Keegan

★ Jeremy Clarkson (really, *really* sorry about this).

★ Also *Vicar of Dibley* actress Emma Chambers, but she 'doesn't like to talk about it'.

PRESTON

> **Playlist**
>
> ▷ **Cornershop** – Brimful Of Asha

FAVOURITE FACTS

➤ There are so many impressive things about Preston
I don't know where to start. For instance, we've had
lots of firsts:
1 The first stretch of motorway
2 We had the first KFC (in the UK that is – there
was probably at least one in Kentucky before
we got ours).
3 We were the first town outside London to be
lit by gas.
4 Preston North End FC were the first winners
of the double (1889–90).
5 The first traffic cones were here too!

➤ We've got the tallest church spire in England:
St Walburge's.

➤ And we've got a nuclear power plant called Springfield,
just like in *The Simpsons*!

➤ In the early twentieth century Preston had 365 pubs,
one for each day of the year.

****

LOCAL HEROES

★ Kenny Baker, who played R2D2, lives round the corner from my mum and dad!

★ Nick Park (*Wallace and Gromit*).

★ Andrew Flintoff, Sir Tom Finney and John Inman ('I'm free!').

★ Cornershop were formed whilst at UCLAN.

CHORLTON -CUM-HARDY

TOASTER: RACHAEL RICHARDS

Playlist

▷ **Doves** – Some Cities (the guitarist drinks in my local, and I have a crush on him!)

FAVOURITE FACTS

← *Postman Pat*, *Count Duckula* and *Dangermouse* were all created here, at Cosgrove Hall Animation Studios. That's enough for you, surely?

← No? Well then, prior to their departure for Australia in 1958, the Bee Gees spent nearly eight years of their childhood living in 51 Keppel Road, Chorlton.

LOCAL HEROES

★ Badly Drawn Boy lives around the corner from me.

TOXTETH

TOASTER: HANNAH MADDEN

Playlist

▷ **CSS** – Music Is My Hot Hot Sex (a tenuous link to the Toxteth Riots in July 1981. During the riots the police employed CS gas for the first time in the UK outside Northern Ireland. And CS gas sounds a bit like CSS…)

FAVOURITE FACTS

- We've got the Williamson Tunnels, a series of tunnels that were dug under Liverpool for no reason whatsoever by a rich and eccentric businessman. (It's thought he was being charitable and trying to find work for local men.) They stretch for miles, and long stretches of them are now open to the public.

- The local by-law that only a clerk in a tropical fish store is allowed to be publicly topless in Liverpool came third as UK's most absurd law in a recent UKTV poll. It was then very sadly confirmed by the City Council that this was a hoax.

- Liverpool has Europe's longest-established Chinese community and Europe's largest Chinese arch, which stands 14 metres over the entrance to Chinatown.

****

LOCAL HEROES

★ Alex Cox, director of *Repo Man* and *Sid and Nancy*.

★ Billy Fury.

★ Holly Johnson of Frankie Goes To Hollywood.

★ Willy Russell, author of the long-running musical
  Blood Brothers.

★ Ringo Starr

LOCAL ANTIHERO

↓ Alois Hitler Jr lived in upper Stanhope Street. Half-brother
  to Adolf, who is said to have come to stay in 1912–13!

STOCKPORT

TOASTERS: OLIVIA HOWITT
GILLIAN DONOVAN

Playlist

▷ **The Housemartins** – Bow Down

▷ **Half Man Half Biscuit** – Light At The End Of The Tunnel
(Is The Light Of An Oncoming Train)

FAVOURITE FACTS

➤ Stockport was once at the centre of the British hatting
industry – in 1884 more than 6 million hats a year were
being exported. The town's hatting heritage can be
found at Hat Works – The Museum of Hatting. It has
a café, if you're thinking of coming.

➤ Due to a Parliamentary Act in 1840 in order to get
Stockport's viaduct built all passenger trains using the
structure had to stop at the station by law. Even today
all London trains stop at Stockport station.

➤ Stockport's Merseyside Shopping Centre is built on
stilts over the River Mersey, which spans the entirety
of the complex – because of this Waterstone's cannot
have a lift.

➤ The Moolah Rouge recording studios in Davenport just
outside of Stockport is or has been home to names such

as: I Am Kloot, Badly Drawn Boy, Cherry Ghost, Doves, Johnny Marr, Happy Mondays, Stephen Fretwell, The Cribs, The Verve and Bez.

- Olivia: I sang backing vocals on the Housemartins track 'Bow Down' when I was in the Saint Winifred's School Choir. The choir was famous for the Christmas number one in 1980: 'There's No One Quite Like Grandma'. I think it ran for two weeks.

LOCAL HEROES

★ Roisin Murphy went to school in Stockport. I took her Saturday job in a shop called Crazy Face when she left.

★ Mrs Merton started on a local Stockport radio, KFM, with Craig Cash. The programme *Mrs Merton and Malcolm* was based in Heaton Norris, Stockport.

★ Dominic Monaghan from *Lost* and *Lord of the Rings*.

★ Dominic Howard, Muse drummer.

★ Tim McInnerny of *Blackadder* fame.

SCUNTHORPE

TOASTER: ANN DEARY

Playlist

▷ **The Undertones** – Teenage Kicks
(in honour of John Peel)

FAVOURITE FACTS

- The town's motto is 'The Heavens reflect our labours'.
This alludes to the glow above the steelworks and
suggests Scunthorpe may be the only town in the world
to find civic pride in how polluted they are.

- Every McDonald's burger in the UK is made in Scunthorpe
at the McKey's factory.

- John Peel used to take his roadshow to Scunthorpe on
an annual basis. The venue was Scunthorpe Baths – the
original dancefloor was on top of the empty pool, giving

it the accidental effect of the sprung dancefloors popular in Northern Soul clubs.

- The mascot of Scunthorpe United (SUFC – aka The Iron) is the 'Scunny Bunny'. The 'softness' of this mascot is held responsible for recent bad form of SUFC. Locals are currently petitioning to have it changed to the more ferocious 'Iron Lion'.

LOCAL HEROES

★ Joan Plowright and Liz Smith (*The Royle Family*) were born in Scunny. Rumours abound that Donald Pleasance also lived in the town.

★ Graeme Taylor, Ray Clemence, Ian Botham and Kevin Keegan all started their sporting careers playing at SUFC.

TOAST
NORTHERN
IRELAND

DERRY

TOASTER: ROISIN O'DOHERTY

Playlist

▷ **Pink Floyd** – The Wall (Derry is the only remaining unbreached walled city in UK)

FAVOURITE FACTS

- Derry was founded by St Columba or Colmcille, and the name translates as Oak Grove.

- The shirt factory industry in the mid-1800s was so famous it was mentioned in *Das Kapital* by Karl Marx.

- Derry entered *The Guinness Book of Records* in 2007 for the biggest gathering of Santas – 13,000 in the one place, beating London and Las Vegas!

- There has always been a dispute about whether the city's name is Derry or Londonderry. A local radio presenter has named it Stroke City instead, and it has kind of stuck. It's often also known as the Maiden City – some reckon this is because of the unbreached walls, others say it's due to the unusually high number of virgins living here!

- Derry has the steepest main street in Europe, called Shipquay Street. Because of its extreme hilliness, people on the waterside are said have developed a special kind of walk!

****

LOCAL HEROES

★ Martin O'Neill

★ The Undertones

★ Neil Hannon – Divine Comedy.

★ Nadine Coyle

★ Bronagh Gallagher – *The Commitments* and *Pulp Fiction*.

★ Dana, Eurovision winner.

★ Baltimora – 'Tarzan Boy'!

★ George Farquhar

★ Roma Downey

★ Amanda Burton

★ Phil Coulter, Svengali to The Bay City Rollers and writer of 'Puppet On A String'.

★ John Hume

BELFAST

'PRO TANTO QUID RETRIBUAMUS:
WHAT SHALL WE GIVE IN RETURN FOR SO MUCH'
Town motto

How brave and upfront of Toaster Margaret to deliver the bad news first re: her home city of Belfast by saying right at the off: yes, it was us wot made the *Titanic*!' Obfuscating the fact or burying it beyond other great facts about the Kelvin scale and Van Morrison would have been the radio equivalent of an estate agent proclaiming airily, 'Oh, so you've *noticed* the nuclear power station at the bottom of the back yard?'

Something that never fails to shock me about this Toast the Nation feature is just how little I know about these British Isles I claim to be a part of. For instance, I had *no idea* that Belfast's City Airport was renamed after George Best! One has to ruminate on that for a moment and conclude that it is a slightly bizarre match, that of an international airport and a fallen footballer who sadly drank himself to death. That said, the more I think about it the more it makes sense. Surely, THE ONLY PLACE IN THE WORLD you can drink at 9 a.m. *without* being considered an alcoholic is an international airport? For that reason alone, it seems fitting. In that, ahem, spirit, I look forward to the renaming of JFK Airport to the David Hasselhoff Airport, and Charles De Gaulle Airport to *L'aéroport de Gérard Depardieu*.

****

R2D2 LIVES IN PRESTON

TOASTER: MARGARET O'HARE

Playlist

▷ **David Holmes** – I Heard Wonders
(he was born in Belfast)

▷ **Van Morrison** – Bright Side Of The Road

▷ **Wolfman (ft. Pete Doherty)** – For Lovers

FAVOURITE FACTS

- The *Titanic*, of course, that's us. We did her. (In 1900 Belfast had the biggest shipyard, rope makers and textile factory in the world.)

- Belfast also brought you the Kelvin scale of absolute temperature, via Lord William Kelvin. It's also home to the oldest English-language newspaper in the world still in print, the *Newsletter*.

****

- The last wolf in Ireland was killed here.

- It has cracking bars, magic people, the craic is ninety. A veritable smorgasbord of restaurants and cafés. Will personally guarantee a good night out if you get yourselves over here. Forget Dublin, you can't afford it anyway. Especially with the euro the way it is . . .

- Belfast is the easiest town to leave and the easiest town to come back to, as a wise old sage said.

LOCAL HEROES

★ We love Georgie Best so much we've named an airport after him.

★ Van Morrison is another famous son, as was.

★ C. S. Lewis

★ Actors Kenneth Branagh, Stephen Rea and Ciaran Hinds come from here.

★ Liam Neeson and Jimmy Nesbit hail from just outside Belfast.

TOAST
SCOTLAND

GLASGOW

**'THERE ARE SOME OF US LUCKY
ENOUGH TO BE GLASWEGIAN.
THE REST OF YOU JUST WANNABE...'**

Glasgow. Its feet washed by the banks of the Clyde. Source of the Scottish Enlightenment. Proud builder of ships and home to some of the greatest artists, writers and thinkers of all time. Of it, Daniel Defoe said, 'it is the cleanest and beautifullest, and best built city in Britain, London excepted' (faint praise if ever I heard it). People come from all over the world to enjoy its architecture and culture. But in the mid-nineties, four young festival goers eschewed the impressive sights and instead went in search of intoxicating spirits. It was 1996, the T in the Park Festival was on in nearby Hamilton, and myself, my brother Paul, Uncle Orms and flatulent friend Chris visited numerous off-licences, diligently calculating the lowest-priced, highest-alcohol-percentage beverage on the market. One shop was doing a nice line in broken wine boxes. They were selling bags of wine (the foil bags from inside the tapped boxes, a mainstay of many a middle-class do of the eighties) for £5 each. That's five quid for THREE LITRES of borderline-undrinkable wine, the equivalent of four bottles for a fiver!

Being both amateur sommeliers and keen bargain hunters, we swooped up their stock and alighted to the campsite, where we could be seen for the rest of the weekend sucking from the foil sacks as they rested under our armpits. Many native Glaswegians took this as a lampoon of their beloved national instrument, the bagpipe (especially as the bag began to empty and we had to work the foul tipple up the pipe via an arm-pumping action), but luckily none of us were assaulted.

It was during this particular festival that, during the climactic dénouement of their most famous song, Jarvis of Pulp pointed directly toward me as I rested on Orms's shoulders and bellowed, 'I wanna be with common people . . . Like YOU!' I felt vindicated, anointed, and accepted. After all, what could be more common than sucking cheap wine out of a foil bag on a campsite?

TOASTERS: RAB RODGERS
ELLIE CADDELL
LENA

Playlist

▷ **Alex Harvey** – Last Of The Teenage Idols
(he's from Glasgow)

▷ **Teenage Fan Club** – Don't Look Back

▷ **Franz Ferdinand** – Outsiders

FAVOURITE FACTS

- The grid street pattern of Manhattan is a scaled-up version of Glasgow city centre, where it was tried first.

- According to a study from *Men's Health* magazine in 2006, Glasgow is the most dangerous, lazy and drunk city in Britain.

****

- Irn-Bru is a soft drink that is more popular here than Coca-Cola. When one of the popular fast-food takeaway places opened in Glasgow and did not sell Irn-Bru, it was considered an insult, and the restaurant was boycotted.

> **SHAUN SEZ:** Remember the eighties strapline for Irn-Bru, beloved of kids up and down the country? 'IRN-BRU, MADE IN SCOTLAND, FROM GIRRRR-DERRRS!' Of course, the drink is NOT made from metal girders, nor does drinking it immediately make one immensely hard or strong. You DO get a bit burpy, though.

- In Glasgow you must always look up – to appreciate the stunning architecture. Glasgow has an impressive heritage of Victorian buildings, including the Glasgow City Chambers; the main building of the University of Glasgow, and the Kelvingrove Art Gallery and Museum.

- There are more pubs in Glasgow than people.

- Glasgow Celtic were the first BRITISH team to win the European Cup, in 1967! Perhaps more impressively, they're the only club in history to have won the European Cup with a team comprised entirely of home-grown players (all born and bred within a 30-mile radius of the stadium).

LOCAL HEROES

* Billy Connolly, comedian.

* Robert Carlyle – played a Bond villain in *The World is Not Enough* and Begbie in *Trainspotting*.

* Sir Thomas Lipton – of tea and shop fame (created Lipton's Tea).

* Alex Harvey – Sensational Alex Harvey Band.

* Frankie Miller, singer.

* Alex Ferguson

* Kenny Dalglish – has managed Blackburn, Newcastle, Liverpool and Celtic.

* Tony Blair's granny – but we don't talk about that much!

* The Jesus And Mary Chain

* Camera Obscura

* Belle & Sebastian

* Sons & Daughters

* Teenage Fanclub

EDINBURGH

Edinburgh. It's built on a giant rock. The rock is actually comprised mostly of granite, not crack cocaine as was implied in that great Edinburgh Tourist Board-endorsed snapshot of the city, *Trainspotting*. That Ewan MacGregor! He can even look sexy after a year on the horse, crawling out of a faeces-filled toilet!

Irvine Welsh's unflinchingly nihilistic, narcotic look at the city aside, what does our Toaster, Charles Roper, have to say about Scotland's capital? Well, he reminds us that Edinburgh is the ultimate New Year's Eve party capital, and that it hosts one of the world's most prestigious and popular arts festivals. But my favourite fact is that none other than Sir Sean Connery used to do a milk round in the city. How cool? After hearing that fact I couldn't help but fantasize how great it would be if, rather than retire to a distant Caribbean isle with his millions, Sean returned to his home city, and to the very milk round that he abandoned for a life of international film stardom . . .

(Interlude of that tinkling harp music that denotes someone slipping into a daydream.)
Doorbell.
SIR SEAN: Hello, the name is Bond. James Bond.
HOUSEHOLDER: Can I get some double cream today please, Sean?
SIR SEAN: It doesn't matter how much you torture me, Blofeld, I will never talk!
HOUSEHOLDER: And we won't be needing any milk next week, we're off on holiday.

****

SIR SEAN: I'll just make a note of that with this pen, which is also a BOMB!
HOUSEHOLDER: I'm going to go inside now, Sean. By the way there are some kids nicking bottles off the back of your milk float.
SIR SEAN: You mean my Aston Martin?
HOUSEHOLDER: Goodbye.

TOASTER: CHARLES ROPER

Playlist

▷ **Iggy Pop** – Lust For Life (as it's in the opening sequence of *Trainspotting*, when they charge along Princes Street)

▷ **Broken Records** – If The News Makes You Sad Don't Watch It

▷ **K. T. Tunstall** – Miniature Disasters

FAVOURITE FACTS

☛ The name comes from Din Eidyn, which means 'Edwin's fort', and translates into English as Edinburgh. It has been capital of Scotland since 1437.

☛ Leith is part of Edinburgh but still retains a separate identity. For years, it had separate licensing laws, leading to our most famous pub, the Boundary Bar, which had one door in Leith and one in Edinburgh.

****

It used to have two separate closing times due to different licensing laws, so at 10.30 everyone would cram from one bar into the other. Leith is twinned with Rio de Janeiro.

- The Edinburgh Fringe Festival is the largest performing arts festival in the world.

SHAUN SEZ: Many confused hairdressers have turned up at Edinburgh over the years ready to showcase their latest fringe flourishes, to be sadly disappointed.

- Rockstar North, the video games makers who created Lemmings and Grand Theft Auto, are based here.

- There are a number of cafés that claim to be the birthplace of the speccy boy wizard, as J. K. wrote in cafés to save on heating as she was broke. Not any more. *Forbes* has named Rowling as the first person to become a US-dollar billionaire by writing books.

LOCAL HEROES

★ Sir Arthur Conan Doyle

★ Ian Rankin, creator of Inspector Rebus.

★ Irvine Welsh, who illustrated the less pleasant side of Edinburgh life in *Trainspotting* and other books, lives here.

★ J. K. Rowling

****

- ★ Ian Anderson out of Jethro Tull grew up in Edinburgh (and is my cousin).

- ★ Sir Sean Connery was a milkman down the road, although it is said that, if every granny in Edinburgh who claims he was their milkman is telling the truth, he must have delivered milk at about 200 mph.

- ★ The Proclaimers – based in Leith.

- ★ The Bay City Rollers

- ★ K. T. Tunstall

GREENOCK

'FOR AYE THE NAME O' GREENOCK TOON
SHALL STILL BE DEAR TO ME'
Traditional poem

TOASTER: STUART MCKECHNIE

Playlist

▷ **Men At Work** – Down By The Sea

▷ **Blood Red Shoes** – Its Getting Boring By The Sea

▷ **Echo & The Bunnymen** – Seven Seas

▷ **Modest Mouth** – Ocean Breathes Salty

▷ **The Futureheads** – Back To The Sea

(You can probably spot they're all sea-related.)

FAVOURITE FACTS

- Greenock lies on the south bank of the Clyde at the 'Tail of the Bank', where the River Clyde expands into the Firth of Clyde, and is in what was the county of Renfrewshire. We are twinned with Duisburg, Germany.

- Abdelbaset Ali Mohmed Al Megrahi lived here. Otherwise known as the Lockerbie Bomber. And by lived, I mean he was in the prison we have.

****

- Greenock is home for both Scotland's longest railway tunnel (1.2 miles) and Scotland's oldest evening newspaper, which is also one of the UK's oldest daily local papers.

- The local ship builders helped to construct the *QE2* and to build ships during the Second World War as well. This made the area a target of Nazi bombing campaigns.

LOCAL HEROES

★ The town's most notable resident was James Watt, the inventor of the modern steam engine.

★ Richard Wilson – *One Foot in the Grave*.

★ US chat show host Jay Leno's mum.

★ Lawrence Tynes, the kicker for the New York Giants, was born and raised here.

ALLOA

**'SCOTLAND'S SMALLEST COUNTY
[WITH] ITS SIGHTS SET HIGH'**

clacksweb.com

TOASTER: BARRY DUFF

Playlist

▷ **Jason Webley** – The Drinking Song

▷ **Bad Manners** – Special Brew

▷ **The Pogues** – Streams Of Whisky

▷ **Thrum** – Here I Stand

▷ **Goldfrapp** –Train

FAVOURITE FACTS

➤ The county motto is 'Look aboot ye', apparently inspired by King Robert the Bruce, who said it when he lost a glove while on a hunting trip. The glove was found where the town Clackmannan now stands, just outside Alloa.

- Alloa is the main town in Clackmannanshire, the smallest region in Scotland. Hence it is called 'The Wee County'.

- Alloa was a major brewery town, second only to Edinburgh in production. There used to be nine major breweries in the town, but only one small family brewery survives. It makes a drink called Fraoch, which is an ale made from heather. It tastes just as good as it sounds!

- Alloa Tower dates from the fourteenth century and was home for the Earls of Mar. Legend has it that Mary Queen of Scots' infant son, James VI of Scotland (who would become James I of England) died and was replaced with the Earl's own son. The tower still stands. It is a gorgeous building, unfortunately now situated right next to a giant Tesco.

- The biggest news to hit Alloa recently was the train link to Glasgow reopening last year after forty years out of use.

LOCAL HEROES

★ Alan Hansen (Liverpool and Scotland international footballer and *Match of the Day* pundit).

★ Daniel Defoe (author of *Robinson Crusoe*) is from Sauchie, a small town next to Alloa.

COATBRIDGE

Let me make something perfectly clear right here and now. This book, is no 'Crap Towns'. Indeed not. It's unlikely to sell anywhere near that number of copies for a start, partly because people like to SLAG THINGS OFF! Me included. Despite that, this book is quite the opposite of Crap Towns. It is a rapturous celebration of this United Kingdom in which we are lucky to reside. It is a lengthy love letter to the towns, cities and hamlets that grace its pages. All that said, I would be worse than one of Orwell's Ministers of Information if I blithely erased from history the opinions and facts of some of our less celebratory listeners. One such man is Buck Smith, Toaster of the Scottish town of Coatbridge. The picture he paints of his hometown is less postcard, more test card. He gleefully reports that Coatbridge has achieved the civic medal of honour that is the Carbuncle Award (the Oscars for Scotland's most disgusting new buildings), and he cites the Time Capsule, an adventure swimming pool and ice rink set in a prehistoric environment, as one of the town's few jewels in the crown. I was all ready to make some withering comments about this ambitious-sounding water-based leisure complex, until I looked it up on the 'inter-net'.

My, what a place it looks! Were such a place available to me as a nine-year-old willow-limbed water waif I would surely have died of the first ever case of chlorinated-water poisoning! They'd have had to fish me out forcibly with an oversize carp net. The place has a rubber ring-ride! And a flume! A FLUME! If there is *any* leisure pursuit on offer to the contemporary adult that comes CLOSE to providing the level of giddy ecstasy a swimming pool containing inflatables and chutes does to a child, I have yet to uncover it. That said, I am yet to attend one of those high-class central London masked swingers' events, so perhaps my judgement should be reserved.

TOASTER: BUCK SMITH

Playlist

▷ **The Pogues** – Dirty Old Town (captures the town covered in smog from the iron foundries and of course the Irish influence on the place)

FAVOURITE FACTS

☞ A favourite attraction is the Time Capsule, an adventure swimming pool and ice rink set in a prehistoric environment.

- Coatbridge was an industrial town and was a centre of the steel and iron industry back in the nineteenth century. The town was known as the 'Iron Burgh'.

- Summerlee Heritage Park boasts that it is Scotland's Noisiest Museum. It pays homage to iron and steel industry in the town, with many working parts of machinery, as well as tram cars and steam engines.

- Coatbridge won the Carbuncle Award 2007 for being Scotland's most dismal place to live.

LOCAL HEROES

★ Dean Ford, lead singer of Marmalade.

> **SHAUN SEZ:** Did they ever support The Jam? Other great spread-rock bands? Har Marmite Superstar? NutElla Fitzgerald? Airto and Flora? 2-LurPac Shakur? Sorry...

★ Comic book writer Mark Millar, who has written *Marvel*, *Wanted*, *The Authority*, *Fantastic Four* and *Spider-Man*.

★ Sisters Fran and Anna, a traditional Scottish music duo.

★ Des Dillon, writer and poet – *Me and My Gal*, *The Big Empty*.

DRYMEN

TOASTER: AMY

Playlist

▷ **The Kinks** – Village Green Preservation Society

FAVOURITE FACTS

- Rob Roy used to frequent Drymen – his aunt owned a pub which is still running and claims to be the oldest pub in Scotland – established in 1734.

LOCAL HEROES

★ Billy Connolly used to live here.

★ Noel Edmonds was married (in 1986) in Drymen.

★ Eric Liddel (of *Chariots of Fire* fame) spent his summer holidays in Drymen as a kid.

FALKIRK

TOASTER: MARC WRIGHT

Playlist

▷ **Glasvegas** – Careful What You Wish For

FAVOURITE FACTS

- Falkirk is the only settlement in Great Britain to have a name in four languages: Egglesbreth in English (previous name); Falkirk (or Fawkirk) in Scots; La Chapelle de Fayerie in French; An Eaglais Bhreach in Scottish Gaelic.

- The Falkirk Wheel (the world's first rotating boat lift), which joins the Forth and Clyde Canal with the Union Canal, uses the same amount of electricity to rotate as it takes to boil a kettle!

LOCAL HEROES

★ James Allen, lead singer of Glasvegas, used to play for Falkirk FC.

★ Malcolm Middleton and Aidan Moffat from Arab Strap are from here.

★ John Logie Baird, although he first worked on the idea in Hastings (see p. 93), perfected and demonstrated the first television set in Falkirk.

****

FETTERCAIRN

TOASTER: KATH BAIRD

Playlist

▷ **Rilo Kiley** – Portions For Foxes
(because of the hunting connection)

▷ **Thin Lizzy** – Whiskey In The Jar

FAVOURITE FACTS

➤ There's lots of hunting and shooting with several country
estates in the area – the place is rife with suicidal pheasants
which dash onto the roads at the least provocation.

➤ Fettercairn is a small village in north-east Scotland.
It has existed in some form or other for over 1,000 years.

****

- Queen Victoria and Prince Albert stayed for one whole night in September 1861. It was supposed to be a secret, but the villagers found out and promptly built a stone arch to celebrate the event, with typical Scots over-reaction.

- It's a biker's Mecca, as it nestles against the Cairn O'Mount, which has some fantastic roads going over to Banchory – it's also often mentioned on travel bulletins as it is one of the first roads to be closed when it snows in the east.

- It has a distillery which opened in 1824 and still produces whisky today (Old Fettercairn).

CUMBERNAULD

TOASTER: GORDON DAY

> **Playlist**
>
> ▷ **Monty Python** – Always Look On The Bright Side Of Life

FAVOURITE FACTS

- Cumbernauld was voted officially the ugliest building in the UK in 2005. This vote referred to the entire town centre, which is all part of one huge concrete complex.

- What's more, Pontius Pilate was reputedly born here! Beat that! Without him the world's best-selling novel wouldn't have had the cliff-hanging ending it did, and Monty Python would have been robbed of some of their funniest gags (Fwee Woddewick).

LOCAL HEROES

★ Jon Fratelli

★ Craig Ferguson – used to be a comedian on British TV (do you remember the comedy series *Absolutely*?), now an American chat show host.

★ Neil Primrose from Travis.

****

PENCAITLAND

TOASTER: CLAIRE HALL

> **Playlist**
>
> ▷ **Edwyn Collins** – Coffee Table Song (the first Orange
>   Juice singles were recorded in my village)

FAVOURITE FACTS

- Renowned duo The Krankies recorded the Scotland
  World Cup anthem, 'We're Going To Spain', in the village
  in 1982, ably assisted in the chorus by my friend Roger
  and his primary-school classmates. This track made it
  onto what has to be the most pointless record in history,
  the Keith Chegwin-fronted *Cheggers' Choice: The Worst
  Album On The Planet '40 Clucking Awful Tracks'*.

LOCAL HEROES

★ The most unusual people ever to have lived in the
  village are probably my parents, a sculptor and a potter.
  In the early eighties, disillusioned with state education,
  they started a school with some friends, which lasted
  five years.

STIRLING

TOASTER: DAVE CARBERY

Playlist

▷ **Arcade Fire** – Intervention (well . . . uh . . . there's a fine Victorian shopping mall in Stirling called The Arcade. And I can imagine that at some point a local yob will have thought about burning it down, and if they did the local constabulary would have to intervene)

FAVOURITE FACTS

➤ Stirling mostly missed bombing during the Second World War. The only place that was bombed was the football ground of the then local team, Kings Park FC, and it put them out of business.

- You can see four famous battlefields from Stirling Castle.

- Apparently, the 'ubiquitous' chewing-gum-removal machine was invented in Stirling.

- The Stirling Jug was the liquid measure to which all other Scottish measures were standardized. It was instituted in 1457 and was not superseded until imperial measures were introduced in 1707.

LOCAL HEROES

★ Billy Bremner (my mum was at school with him!).

ACKNOWLEDGEMENTS

Thanks to Louise Orchard, the genius behind the name TOAST THE NATION; James Stirling for hours of feature-related rumination; Nic 'Philpsy' Philps; Matt Everitt (yes, the one who was in Menswear); Lisa Kenlock; Paul Rodgers; Mike Hanson; Zoe Fletcher and Richard Berry; Caroline Hunt; Claire Hudson; Lewis Carnie; Bob Shennan; Andy 'Kizzle' Hipkiss; Dusty, Jon, Tania, Amy, Matt (for the great illustrations) and Bruno from Boxtree; my parents, without whom, etc.; my myriad of northern mates for providing, and making, many memories; our Orms (yes, he is my uncle. I KNOW it's weird that he's only two years older than me!); our kid; my mother-in-law Carol for her publishing-related support; my adoring and adored wife Lucy; King Arthur; and most of all me, without whom this entire project would have been uncompleted.

****

INDEX

****

****

****

Shaun Keaveny and BBC 6 Music would like to thank all the contributors to Toast the Nation since it began, and especially those whose contributions are included in this book. We've done our best to check that all contributors' names are correct, but if any errors have been included the publishers will be happy to correct them in all future editions and can be contacted at the address on page iv of this book.

**THINK THAT YOUR HOMETOWN
SHOULD HAVE BEEN TOASTED?**

Get stuck in and join the debate!

www.toastthenation.com